A-Z

of OMBUDSMEN

A guide to Ombudsman schemes in Britain and Ireland

National **Consumer** Council

Published by the National Consumer Council

Published by the National Consumer Council
20 Grosvenor Gardens
London SW1W 0DH

Telephone   0171 730 3469
Fax   0171 730 0191

Research by Jane Vass, independent
researcher and writer, London.
Design by Designer Jack, London.
Printed by Russell Press, Nottingham.

ISBN 1 899581 06 5

July 1997

FOREWORD

In both public and private sectors, 'ombudsmania' should be rampant.

Ombudsman schemes provide members of the public with an affordable remedy where otherwise there would be none. And it is not only the complainant who gains - those complained about find that providing a thorough and fair avenue of redress has beneficial influences on their image, customer relations and internal practices.

Of course, for Ombudsmen to be successful, people need to know of their existence and understand how they operate. That is why I heartily welcome this first detailed guide to Ombudsmen by the National Consumer Council. It provides the public and those who advise them with the information they need to get maximum advantage from Ombudsman schemes.

What about the future? I would like Ombudsmen to be given wider scope to take on matters which now have to be resolved by the courts. They should be able to ask the courts to clarify points of law on the basis of evidence gathered during ombudsman investigations, without need of a formal trial. Conversely, courts should be able to ask Ombudsmen to investigate issues of fact on the courts' behalf.

Clearly, there is great scope to expand both the numbers and role of Ombudsmen. But growth must go hand in hand with quality controls. That is why I commend the efforts of the British and Irish Ombudsman Association to set criteria for ombudsman schemes, and to identify and share good practice.

The Rt. Hon., the Lord Woolf,

Master of the Rolls

Foreword

(iii)   The Rt. Hon., the Lord Woolf,
         Master of the Rolls

Introduction

(vi)   David Hatch CBE JP, Chairman,
         National Consumer Council

How to use this guide

(viii)

CONTENTS

Banks and Building Societies

1   Office of the Banking Ombudsman

14   Building Societies Ombudsman

26   Ombudsman for the Credit
         Institutions

Broadcasting

37   Broadcasting Standards
         Commission

Estate Agents

47   Ombudsman for Corporate Estate
         Agents

Funerals

59   Funeral Ombudsman

Government

69   Parliamentary Ombudsman

82   Northern Ireland Ombudsman

94   Office of the Ombudsman,
         Republic of Ireland

Health

107   Health Service Ombudsman

Housing

    119   Independent Housing Ombudsman

    133   The Housing Association Ombudsman for Scotland

Insurance

    143   Insurance Ombudsman Bureau

    156   Insurance Ombudsman of Ireland

Investments

    167   Office of the Investment Ombudsman

    177   Personal Investment Authority Ombudsman Bureau

Legal services

    193   Legal Services Ombudsman for England and Wales

    204   Scottish Legal Services Ombudsman

Local Government

    213   Local Government Ombudsman for England

    227   Local Government Ombudsman for Scotland

    238   Local Government Ombudsman for Wales

Pensions

    251   Pensions Ombudsman

Prisons

    265   Prisons Ombudsman

    276   The Scottish Prisons Complaints Commission

Police

    285   Police Complaints Authority

    297   Independent Commission for Police Complaints in Northern Ireland

Taxes and National Insurance

    309   Adjudicator for Inland Revenue, Customs and Excise and Contributions Agency

INTRODUCTION

In an ideal world problems are prevented before they happen. But it's a fact that consumers and product or service providers end up at loggerheads from time to time. The key consumer test when that happens is whether there's a system for putting things right.

It is heartening that in Ombudsman schemes, consumers now have access to a growing number of impartial referees, across a wide range of public and private organisations. In the thirty years since the first Ombudsman was established in Britain, enthusiasm for this way of resolving disputes has spawned as many as twenty-seven different schemes in Britain and Ireland.

Nowhere else in the world is there such a large network of Ombudsman schemes. To ensure their reputation for integrity and thoroughness, in 1993 the existing Ombudsmen established an association to set standards for all its members. The British and Irish Ombudsman Association, as it is now called, ensures that its member schemes are independent, accessible, fair and accountable to the public.

Sadly, however, many people are only vaguely aware that Ombudsmen exist - and few have any idea of what they actually do. Even the very best informed consumers report difficulties in working out which particular Ombudsman to contact about a problem.

That is why we have put together this guide. We make no comment on any particular scheme's quality, effectiveness or successes. Our aim is to provide a tool that gives ready access to information about the Ombudsman network, what the schemes cover and how consumers can use them to best effect.

We have kept the busy advice worker uppermost in our minds. Ombudsman schemes exist first and foremost to help consumers with grievances they have been unable to resolve themselves. We have tried to present the information collected here in a format which is clear and easy to use - and hope the guide will become an essential item in advisers' consumer kit bags.

The information should also be useful to Ombudsmen themselves - in their second job of working to improve standards generally in the service, department or industry in which they work. We hope they will find the guide a useful source of information about how their colleagues operate. Students of Ombudsman schemes, too, will find it a useful reference.

We are extremely grateful for the help the Ombudsmen and their staff have given us in putting the guide together - not least for their unflagging patience with our epic questionnaire and endless follow-up questions.

We hope you find it useful.

David Hatch CBE JP

Chairman, National Consumer Council

HOW TO USE THIS GUIDE

This guide is designed to provide advice workers with the information they need to respond quickly to queries about Ombudsman schemes. Schemes that operate in similar areas are grouped together in the same section - such as Banks and Building Societies. Each entry begins with the Ombudsman scheme's contact details. E-mail and web site details have been given where we have been told about them. Each entry is then divided into three sections:

1. Using the scheme: key points

This section covers the basics - such as who belongs to the scheme, the kinds of complaint the scheme deals with, how soon a complaint has to be made and what the Ombudsman can do to remedy the situation.

2. The complaints procedure

Here we describe each stage involved between making the complaint and reaching a final resolution.

3. The scheme's structure and administration

This section includes more detailed information about the schemes - such as when and how the scheme was set up, how much it costs to run, and figures on the complaints it has dealt with over the last two years. It also points to other information about the scheme, where there is any.

Office of the Banking Ombudsman

70 Gray's Inn Road, London WC1X 8NB
Tel: 0171 404 9944. Fax: 0171 405 5052
Enquiries: Lo-call 0345 660902
E-mail: banking.ombudsman@obo.org.uk
Web site: http://www.intervid.co.uk./obo

Ombudsman: David Thomas

1. Using the scheme: key points

Service-providers covered

All high street banks in the UK - covering 99% of all retail bank customers.

Complaints covered

Complaints about negligence, maladministration and other breaches of duty (including inequitable treatment) in connection with banking business conducted through branches, telephone, cash machines or bank plastic cards.

(If a UK bank that subscribes to the Code of Banking Practice fails to inform a complainant about the Banking Ombudsman scheme, the Ombudsman can treat this as maladministration.)

Complaints not covered

Complaints about a bank's commercial decisions, like its general interest rate policy, although the Ombudsman can deal with complaints of maladministration in the course of making a commercial decision.

Complaints involving claims of more than £100,000.

Complaints pursued in a frivolous or vexatious manner.

Complaints that have been - or become - subject to court proceedings, unless the bank in question gives its written consent. Once a court or another Ombudsman has ruled on the complaint, the Banking Ombudsman cannot look into it.

Who can complain?

Individuals, partnerships, other unincorporated bodies, and small companies (with an annual turnover of less than £1 million).

The personal representative of a dead person.

Beneficiaries of a dead person's estate.

People who are not direct customers of the bank in question can usually use the scheme - for example, the true owner of a stolen cheque, the recipient of a banker's reference or a guarantor.

Cost

Free to complainants.

Geographical limits

The banking service must have been provided in the UK, but the complaint need not have arisen in the UK. For instance, if a bank provides a plastic card from a UK branch, complaints arising from its use abroad will be eligible.

Complainants do not have to be British or resident in the UK.

Banking services provided from the Channel Islands or the Isle of Man are not covered.

Time limits

The event that gave rise to the complaint must be after the bank in question joined the scheme, and complaints must be brought within 6 years of the event being complained about, unless the complainant could not - using reasonable diligence - have discovered the problem in that time.

A complaint must also be brought within 6 months of reaching deadlock in the bank's internal complaints procedure.

Remedies

Financial compensation

Maximum compensation £100,000. (Average actual award in 1995/96 was £2,815; highest was £56,740.)

Can, and often does, add interest to the compensation for financial loss.

Can compensate for inconvenience, including distress, anxiety and 'hassle', as well as actual financial loss.

Will not usually require a bank to compensate for any legal costs incurred by the complainant, but does occasionally - for instance, where the bank has put the complainant to significant undue trouble and expense, or made it unreasonably necessary for the complainant to instruct a solicitor.

Has the right to reduce the amount of compensation to reflect contributory negligence by the complainant (something a court, under strict contract law, could not do).

2. The complaints procedure

Making the complaint

Complainants can contact the scheme themselves: they do not need to use an intermediary.

Exhausting the internal complaints procedure

The complainant usually has to exhaust the bank's own internal complaints procedure first. The bank must issue a deadlock letter.

When a complaint is brought to the scheme before deadlock has formally been reached, the complainant is referred back to the bank. The bank has 4 weeks either to resolve the complaint or to issue a deadlock letter. If the bank fails to write, or unduly delays writing a deadlock letter, the Ombudsman can decide to investigate without one.

Powers of investigation

Can compel the bank in question to produce any relevant papers.

Cannot compel individuals to attend hearings.

Criteria for decisions

What is fair in all the circumstances.

Any relevant rules of law and previous court decisions.

Good banking practice, based on the Code of Banking Practice and other standards.

The Ombudsman may treat maladministration or other inequitable treatment as a breach of the obligation or duty owed by the bank.

The Ombudsman is not bound by his own (or his predecessors) previous decisions.

Confidentiality

During the investigation, each side may see all of the other side's papers and submissions, except for documents specifically sent in confidence (although these are likely to carry less, if any, weight with the Ombudsman than evidence that is disclosed to the other party). Otherwise all details of a complaint are confidential.

The *Annual Report* publishes anonymous case histories, to illustrate the Ombudsman's decisions.

The complainant can, if he or she chooses, make the Ombudsman's decision public.

Stages in complaint resolution

New complaints

New complaints (and telephone enquiries) are handled by the Complaints Department. If appropriate, informal conciliation will be attempted with eligible complaints.

Complaints where deadlock has not yet been reached are referred back to the bank (see Exhausting the internal complaints procedure above). Complaints that would be better dealt with by another Ombudsman are automatically redirected. The Department screens out complaints that are not eligible or do not show an arguable case, and informs the complainant by letter.   .

Mature complaints

Once deadlock has been reached between the bank and the complainant and if conciliation has failed, eligible cases go on to the Investigation Department. The complainant is asked to complete a complaint form, which includes a waiver of confidentiality to enable the Ombudsman to obtain the necessary papers from the bank. The case is assigned to an adjudicator for a full investigation under the supervision of a team-leader (who will be the Ombudsman, the Deputy Ombudsman or the Assistant Ombudsman).

Investigation

The bank must provide papers and respond within 3 weeks. Cases are largely decided on written evidence. Occasionally, the Ombudsman will interview individuals and/or inspect locations, but there are no formal hearings involving both parties.

Assessment

This is issued at the end of the full investigation. It sets out the facts and gives full reasons for the provisional decision. Most complaints are settled at this stage.

Final decision

If either party does not accept the assessment, the Ombudsman considers any more submissions and/or fresh evidence and then issues a final decision. This is binding on the bank (but not the complainant).

Formal award

> If a bank refuses to accept a formal recommendation, the Ombudsman can make a formal award.

Progress reports

> Complainant and bank are regularly informed about progress.
>
> If a complainant has been waiting for action from the Ombudsman for more than 4 weeks, he or she is usually informed.

Types of ruling

Conciliation

> The scheme works actively to achieve conciliation, particularly before the start of a full investigation but also afterwards. Although the scheme does not keep formal records, the number of preliminary complaints resolved through conciliation is thought to be high.

Assessment

> In the majority of cases decided in favour of the complainant, the bank makes an offer in settlement once an assessment has been issued - and the complainant accepts the offer.

Formal recommendation

> Roughly one-third of cases that are fully investigated reach this stage.

Formal award

> It has never been necessary for the Ombudsman to make a formal award.

Rights of appeal against a decision

> There is no appeal or review stage after the final decision. Complainants who remain dissatisfied can still take their case against a bank to court (though they seldom do in practice).
>
> A recent High Court case (concerning the Insurance Ombudsman Bureau) suggests that the

Banking Ombudsman scheme is not subject to judicial review.

With the Ombudsman's agreement and by promising to pay both sides' legal costs whatever the outcome, a bank can invoke a test case procedure, to enable an important point of law to be referred to the courts. (Only used once in the scheme's lifetime.)

Failure to comply with rulings

Failure of a bank to comply with a Final Decision

The Ombudsman would have to make a Formal Award, which would be binding on the bank.

Failure of a bank to comply with a Formal Award

The bank could be sued by the Board and expelled from the scheme. (This has never been necessary.)

How long does the process take?

Average timescale

From the start of a full investigation to the preliminary decision stage: 193 days in 1995/96 (174 days in 1994/95). Turn-around times are much shorter for complaints that do not need a full investigation.

Urgent complaints are sometimes dealt with more quickly - for example, where a bank seeks to repossess a house.

Delegation of decision-making

All assessments are approved by the Ombudsman, the Deputy Ombudsman or the Assistant Ombudsman. Only the Ombudsman, the Deputy Ombudsman or the Assistant Ombudsman can issue a final decision.

Following up complaints

The outcome of complaints that are outside the scheme's terms of reference are not followed up. When a complaint is sent back to a bank because it has not reached the deadlock stage (see The complaints procedure above), the scheme will continue to offer help.

Whenever the decision is against the bank, the Ombudsman asks for confirmation from both parties that his decision has been complied with.

Complaining about the scheme itself

The scheme has its own internal complaints procedure. Complaints about the scheme are reviewed by the Ombudsman or Deputy Ombudsman. Statistics are not kept.

3. The scheme's structure and administration

Origins and membership

Started operating on 1 January 1986. Set up as an unlimited company not having share capital. Membership is voluntary but is a requirement of the Code of Banking Practice - to which all the UK high street banks subscribe.

Structure and accountability

The scheme is overseen by a Council and a Board.

The Council

Membership

8 members - 5 independent, including the chairman, 3 bank appointees.

Role

The Council safeguards the independence of the Ombudsman; secures adequate funds from the banks; appoints the Ombudsman (subject to the Board's approval) and the Deputy Ombudsman (in consultation with the Ombudsman); receives reports from the Ombudsman about the case-load; and gives general guidance to the Ombudsman. Plays no part in making decisions about individual complaints. Meets quarterly.

The Board

Membership

12 members, all bankers.

Role

The Board agrees the annual budget with the Council; levies the funds from member banks; authorises any changes to terms of reference. Plays no part in making decisions about individual complaints. Meets quarterly.

The Ombudsman

Appointment

By the Council, with Board approval. Can only be dismissed by the Council for misconduct, or on becoming bankrupt or of unsound mind.

Term of appointment

Initially 3 years. Maximum total term: 7 years.

Role

Overall responsibility for running the scheme, including administration and complaints-handling.

Scheme's terms of reference

Established under the articles of association, and amended and up-dated from time to time by the Board, after taking into account recommendations by the Council and the Ombudsman.

Monitoring

None at present.

BIOA member?

Yes.

Funding

Member banks fund the scheme. Each bank pays in proportion to (partly) its retail customer base and (mainly) the number of complaints against it.

Costs

Running cost

£2,204,000 in 1995/96 (£2,077,000 in 1994/95).

Cost per complaint

Not broken down.

Staffing

Overall responsibility

The Ombudsman has overall responsibility for running the office but largely delegates to an administration manager.

Staff

28 operational staff (9 of them part-time) and 13 administrative staff. All but 2 of the adjudicators are legally qualified.

Forthcoming changes

Some changes to the terms of reference are likely.

Improving best practice

The Ombudsman publishes recommendations to the banking industry in his *Annual Report* and sometimes sends guidance letters to all member banks.

Facts and figures

New written complaints (including ineligible complaints)

Subject of complaint	to 30/9/95	to 30/9/96	% change
Lending	1,156	1,382	19.6
Mortgages	775	1,058	36.5
Charges and interest	872	811	-7.0
Account errors	401	447	11.4
Negligence	509	389	-23.6
Insurance	330	329	-0.3
Credit/debit cards	343	324	-5.5
Discourtesy/delay	296	316	6.8
Direct debits/standing orders	313	292	-6.7
ATMs (cash machines)	303	256	-15.5
Opening/closing of account	180	230	27.8
Securities for advances	190	228	20.0
Unauthorised debits (not ATM)	198	200	1.0
Dormant account and destroyed records	134	184	37.3
Multiple complaints	160	178	11.3
Foreign currency and travel	137	132	-3.6
Confidentiality	119	127	6.7
Investment	153	121	-20.9
Cheque guarantee cards	147	120	-18.4
Unwarranted dishonour of cheques	104	116	11.5
Cash dispute (not ATM)	108	107	-0.9
Bankers' references (status opinions)	93	89	-4.3
Executor/trustee and tax	66	75	13.6
Registrar business	37	57	54.1
Safe deposit/custody	15	25	66.7
Fraudulent misrepresentation/ dishonesty	-	8	-
Defamation	-	3	-
Others/unknown	285	440	54.4

Numbers of complaints at each stage of procedure

	to 30/9/95	to 30/9/96	% change
Preliminary complaints received during year	7,424	8,044	8.4
Ineligible complaints (not about a bank)	609	725	19.0
Ineligible complaints (non-member bank)	53	55	3.8
Ineligible complaints (otherwise outside terms of reference)	1,118	1,097	-1.9
Eligible complaints received	5,644	6,167	9.3
Complaints rejected after fast-track decision as involving no breach of duty, loss or inconvenience	1,280	1,053	-17.7
Cases brought forward from previous year	2,223	1,887	-15.1
Cases undergoing further screening (mainly returned to bank)	6,587	7,001	6.3
Cases known to have been settled at the above stage	887	969	9.2
Cases treated as closed (no further contact from complainant). Many were settled	2,227	2,124	-4.6
Cases becoming mature complaints	717	736	2.6
Cases settled during investigation[1]	50	31	-38.0
Preliminary assessments issued[1]	740	557	-24.7
Cases settled on issue of assessment[1]	204	180	-11.8
Formal recommendations issued[1]	253[2]	184	-27.3

Outcome of complaints fully investigated

Favourable to complainant[1]	45%	54%	-
Favourable to bank[1]	55%	46%	-

[1] Includes complaints brought forward from previous year.
[2] Includes one case not settled (a 'test case' taken before the courts).

Information available about the scheme

Publicising the scheme

Banks must inform customers about the scheme if they have a complaint.

Leaflets about the scheme are available in all citizens advice bureaux, other advice agencies and trading standards offices. A range of guidance leaflets is also produced.

The Ombudsman gives lectures and media interviews, and liaises with consumer organisations.

Own Internet web site and Lo-call (0345) telephone enquiry line.

Terms of reference

Available on request.

Annual Report

Published in November/December. Includes breakdowns of types of complaint outside the scheme's terms of reference, numbers of complaints handled, complaints relating to business and personal accounts, and compensation amounts compared to previous bank offers.

Other publications

M. Seneviratne, R. James and C. Graham, 'The Banks, the ombudsman and complaints procedures', *Civil Justice Quarterly*, July 1994.

Laurence Shurman, 'Best laid scheme', *Law Society's Gazette*, 2 March 1994, p. 25.

P.E. Morris, 'The Banking Ombudsman - five years on', *Lloyds Maritime and Commercial Law Quarterly*, 1992, p. 227.

Laurence Shurman, 'What is fair in the relationship between a bank and its customer?' Gilbart Lecture published in *The Banks and Society*, Chartered Institute of Bankers, 1991.

Laurence Shurman, *A Fair Banking Code*, Ernest Sykes Memorial Lecture, Chartered Institute of Bankers, 1991.

Susan M. McAll, *Resolution of Banking Disputes*, chapter 10, Longman , 1990.

P.E. Morris, 'The Banking Ombudsman', *Journal of Business Law,* vol. 131, 1987.

National Consumer Council, *Banking Services and the Consumer*, 1983.

The scheme periodically issues guidance notes to member banks.

Building Societies Ombudsman

Millbank Tower, Millbank, London SW1P 4XS
Tel: 0171 931 0044. Fax: 0171 931 8485

Ombudsman: Brian Murphy

1. Using the scheme: key points

Service-providers covered

All UK building societies and their associated bodies, such as personal loan subsidiaries.

Complaints covered

All complaints must generally relate to the operation or termination of building society accounts.

Complaints of unfair treatment or administrative failure resulting in financial loss or inconvenience.

Complaints that a building society has broken the Building Societies Act 1986, its own rules or any contract.

Complaints not covered

A building society's actions not taken in relation to the complainant personally.

Complaints about creditworthiness - although the Ombudsman has limited powers if, for example, the society fails to use proper credit-rating procedures.

Disputes about a person's rights as a member of a building society.

Complaints about a specialised activity carried out by the building society - for example, estate agency or selling pensions (see sections on estate agents, insurance, investments and pensions).

Complaints without substance and with no reasonable chance of success.

Disputes on which a court has already ruled or are already subject to court proceedings.

Decisions relating to legal action by the building society to enforce its rights.

Who can complain?

Private individuals, groups of individuals and partnerships.

If an account is opened in the name of a private individual as the nominee of an unincorporated body or charity, they too would be able to complain.

Friends, relatives and legal representatives on someone else's behalf, with that person's written authority.

Friends, relatives and legal representatives on behalf of a dead person.

Cost

Free to complainants.

Geographical limits

Can only deal with complaints relating to action taken in the UK (excluding the Channel Islands and Isle of Man).

Time limits

The Ombudsman can decide not to handle a complaint if there has been 'undue delay' by the complainant. In practice, he usually treats as 'undue' an unjustified delay of more than 6 months from the date on which the complainant first became aware that he or she had grounds for complaint (plus any time taken for the complaint to go through a building society's own internal complaints procedure).

Remedies

Financial compensation

Maximum possible award: £100,000 for financial loss, expense or inconvenience. (Highest single award in 1995/96: £52,350.) In practice, the scheme often does not know an award's final cash value - where, for example, the Ombudsman requires a building society to adjust an account, leaving the society to do the calculations.

Can order payment of interest on an award - for instance, if a complainant has wrongly been deprived of the use of his or her money by a society.

Can, and often does, award the costs of legal or other expert advice against a building society, if reasonably incurred by the complainant.

Can, and often does, reduce an award if the complainant's actions contributed to the loss.

Other

For example, restoring an account as it should have been if the problem had not arisen.

2. The complaints procedure

Making the complaint

Complainants can approach the scheme direct. They are invited to put their complaint in writing but oral complaints are acceptable to start the process off. There is a standard complaint form and guidance leaflet. If complainants have difficulty completing the form, an administrator will help, filling it in for them if necessary.

Exhausting the internal complaints procedure

Complainants must first exhaust the building society's own internal complaints procedure. A building society is normally allowed 6 weeks to try to resolve a complaint. If it is not resolved by then, the society should send a formal letter to the Ombudsman, stating that its internal complaints procedures have been exhausted. If the society fails to send such a letter, the Ombudsman will, if requested to do so by the complainant, start his investigation anyway.

If the Ombudsman receives a complaint before internal channels have been exhausted, the complainant gets a letter of explanation and the complaint is sent on to the building society concerned.

Powers of investigation

Can require the complainant or the building society to provide any relevant documents or information.

Criteria for decisions

Codes of practice, good practice and what is fair and reasonable.

The Ombudsman is not strictly bound by his previous decisions: in practice, he always follows them unless it is clear they were wrong.

Confidentiality

During the investigation of a complaint, all documents and other evidence sent in by one party are routinely copied to the other. If either party refuses to allow material to be copied, the Ombudsman will not usually accept it as evidence (indeed, it will be returned unseen by him). The only exception is for commercially sensitive information concerning a society's business or its security arrangements.

Noteworthy decisions are published in the *Annual Report*, but complainants are not identified by name. The building society will sometimes be identified by name, so long as publication would not prejudice, for example, the society's security arrangements.

Stages in complaint resolution

Initial complaints

Complaints officers deal with complaints that have not yet exhausted the building society's internal complaints procedure. They give general advice to the complainant and then pass the complaint to the building society concerned - which has 6 weeks (or occasionally longer) to resolve the complaint through its internal channels.

Initial complaints that appear to be outside the scheme's jurisdiction are referred to the Ombudsman personally: if he decides a complaint is outside his jurisdiction, the complainant is informed. Cases not within the scheme's remit are automatically sent on to another Ombudsman scheme, if appropriate; otherwise, staff help with suggestions wherever possible, such as to contact a citizens advice bureau or law centre.

Investigation

If the complaint cannot be resolved by the building society's internal procedure, the society should inform the Ombudsman. The complaint then becomes a case and investigation starts. Investigation is delegated to a case lawyer, who sends a copy of the complaint to the society concerned, together with detailed questions.

When a response has been received from the building society, the case lawyer considers both the complaint and the society's response and invites either or both sides to submit further evidence, information or argument on any points that are still unclear. The case lawyer then discusses the case in detail with the Ombudsman.

Further investigation and a hearing

If, as sometimes happens, the Ombudsman is not satisfied with the evidence at this stage, he instructs the case lawyer to carry out further investigations. If there is a disagreement about the facts of a complaint, the Ombudsman usually holds an oral hearing, so that he can meet the parties and their witnesses and hear their evidence. Hearings take place in the Ombudsman's office or, if complainants live a long way from London or have difficulty travelling, at a local hotel.

Preliminary decision

The Ombudsman gives his preliminary decision, based on the evidence so far. It is sent to both parties for comment. They are free to agree or disagree with any aspect and to provide further evidence, information and argument. If the preliminary conclusion is accepted by both parties or if the complainant chooses not to proceed any further, the case file will be closed at this stage. Otherwise the Ombudsman reviews the case again in the light of any comments received, before making a final determination.

Final determination

This is sent to both parties. The complainant has 28 days to accept it. (Complainants who do not accept can still take their case to court.) The building society in question must comply with the Ombudsman's final determination, unless it takes the publicity option - explained under Types of ruling below.

Progress reports

The scheme aims to notify complainants about progress, in writing, at each stage.

Types of ruling

Informal conciliation

Around 40% of cases in 1995/96 were settled in this way.

Final decision

This is binding on the building society, unless it elects for the publicity option - outlined below. Final decisions accounted for around 35% of cases in 1995/96.

Publicity option

If the building society does not accept the Ombudsman's final decision, it must publish its reasons for non-compliance in any way the Ombudsman prescribes (such as a press notice).

Rights of appeal against a decision

There is no right of appeal within the scheme. The complainant is still free to pursue a claim through the courts.

It has not been established whether the scheme is subject to judicial review.

Once the complainant has accepted the Ombudsman's decision on any particular case, the building society can require the Ombudsman to refer the case to the High Court to resolve a point of law. (None has so far done so.)

Failure to comply with rulings

The Ombudsman has no contractual powers or sanctions to enforce rulings. (In practice, there has been only one case of non-compliance in the scheme's lifetime, when a building society took the publicity option.)

How long does the process take?

Target timescale

5 months per case (in 1995).

Actual timescale

3.35 months per case, a reduction over the previous year.

If a request for priority from either party is considered reasonable, every effort is made to deal with the complaint as quickly as possible.

Delegation of decision-making

The Ombudsman's powers are not delegated in any way. He signs every final decision letter.

Following up complaints

If a building society fails to confirm that its internal complaints procedure has been exhausted at the end of the time allowed (usually 6 weeks), the Ombudsman will - at the complainant's request - start his investigation.

The Ombudsman does not monitor compliance with his decisions or conduct any other routine follow-up.

Complaining about the scheme itself

Complaints about the scheme are referred to the chairman of the scheme's Council for investigation. (The exact number is not recorded but runs at the rate of about 12 a year; none has been upheld.)

3. The scheme's structure and administration

Origins and membership

Set up to comply with the Building Societies Act 1986, which requires the industry to have an independent complaints-handling mechanism. It was set up as a limited company - The Building Societies Ombudsman Company Ltd. It started operating on 1 July 1987.

Structure and accountability

The scheme is overseen by a Council and a Board.

The Council

Membership

3 industry members, 5 lay members, all appointed by the Board. The chairman is a lay member.

Role

To appoint the Ombudsman (subject to Board approval); to monitor the functioning of the scheme; to approve draft budgets before submitting them to the Board and to ensure that finances are kept within budget; to approve the Ombudsman's *Annual Report*. Plays no role in the resolution of complaints but will give general guidance if the Ombudsman requests it. Meets quarterly.

The Board

Membership

No fewer than 5 or more than 8 industry members, all co-opted. The chairman is an industry member.

Role

To approve budgets and raise funds from all building societies to finance it. The Board has no direct relationship with the Ombudsman and plays no role in the resolution of complaints or the running of the scheme. Meets quarterly.

The Ombudsman

Appointment

By the Council.

Term of appointment

2 years (or longer with Board approval). No limits on the number of re-appointments. Can be removed by the Board (at the request of the Council) without any grounds being specified or if he has an interest which conflicts with his duties.

Role

Overall responsibility for running the office and dealing with complaints.

Scheme's terms of reference

Laid down by statute and set out in the document establishing the scheme. They can be changed by statute or, to a limited extent, by agreement with the industry through the Board.

Monitoring

Performance indicators and standards of service are published in the *Annual Report*.

BIOA member?

Yes.

Funding

Comes from all building societies through the company set up for the purpose. There is an asset-related fee and a case fee per complaint.

Costs

Running cost

£1,498,000 in 1995/96. Costs have been increasing in recent years in line with an increasing workload.

Cost per complaint

Not published.

Staffing

Overall responsibility

Rests with the Ombudsman.

Staff

There are 31 staff. 12 case-handlers (all legally qualified) supervised by the head of legal services. 3 complaints officers (who have a banking background) supervised by a senior case-handling lawyer. 14 support staff supervised by the head of administration.

Forthcoming changes

The Ombudsman is currently awaiting the enforcement of the Building Societies Act 1997 which will extend his jurisdiction so that it is broadly in line with that of the Banking Ombudsman. The legislation would enable the Ombudsman to deal with complaints by small businesses and extend his jurisdiction to include complaints about the provision of services by building societies in the ordinary course of their business (at present limited to complaints about the operation or termination of accounts).

Improving best practice

No specific powers, although the Ombudsman's decisions, summarised in his *Annual Report*, encourage societies to improve their practice. The Ombudsman has regular meetings with the Building Societies Association and also regularly visits building societies, so that he can make his views known on areas of concern.

Facts and figures

Numbers of new complaints received (including ineligible and telephone complaints)

Subject of complaint	1994/95	1995/96	% change
Mortgages	5,859	6,810	16.2
Investments	2,546	2,677	5.1
Miscellaneous	665	709	6.6
Society conversions to public limited companies	667	2,560	284.0
Details unknown	504	277	-45.0

Numbers of complaints at each stage of procedure[1]

	1994/95	1995/96	% change
Total initial complaints and cases handled	10,299	11,375	
Initial complaints not within remit/referred elsewhere	1,958	1,168	
Initial complaints known to have been resolved through society's internal complaints procedure	692	1,116	
Initial complaints not pursued for other reasons[2]	6,286	7147	
Cases resolved after the completion of the internal complaints procedure but before a preliminary conclusion	355	421	18.6
Cases closed following preliminary conclusion accepted by both parties	130	87	-33.0
Cases withdrawn by complainant following an unfavourable preliminary conclusion	173	174	-

Outcome of final determinations

Complaint upheld/upheld in part	363 (51%)	161 (46%)
Complaint not upheld	342 (49%)	189 (54%)

[1] Figures exclude 912 complaints received in 1995/96 concerning the transfer of business from the Cheltenham & Gloucester Building Society to Lloyds Bank.
[2] The vast majority of these complaints do not proceed because there is no action by the complainant.

Information available about the scheme

Publicising the scheme

The Ombudsman requires building societies to inform complainants of the scheme's existence.

There is a guide for applicants and a guidance note for building societies.

Terms of reference

Available on request from the scheme and from building societies.

Annual Report

Normally published in June. Includes detailed breakdown of the subject matter of initial complaints and cases, and further analyses of how they are disposed of.

Ombudsman for the Credit Institutions

8 Adelaide Court, Adelaide Road, Dublin 2
Tel: 00 3531 478 3755. Fax: 00 3531 478 0157

Ombudsman: Gerard Murphy

1. Using the scheme: key points

Service-providers covered

All banks and building societies in the Irish Republic.

Complaints covered

Complaints about unfair treatment, mistakes, administrative failures, negligence, poor service and breach of contract or confidentiality in connection with any type of service.

Complaints not covered

Complaints about a bank's or building society's commercial judgement or policy, unless the complaint concerns unfairness or discrimination in a lending decision.

Complaints about the actions taken by a scheme member using his or her discretion as trustee or executor of a will or trust.

Complaints where the amount in dispute, or which could be awarded, is more than IR£30,000.

Complaints about matters that came to light before 1 October 1990 (or 1 October 1994 for limited companies).

Disputes that are, or have been, the subject of legal proceedings, or that, in the Ombudsman's opinion, would be more appropriately dealt with by a court.

Who can complain?

Individuals, groups of people, businesses, partnerships, charities, unincorporated bodies (such as clubs) and limited companies with an annual turnover of less than IR£250,000 (so long as they are not part of a larger group).

Friends, relatives and legal representatives on someone else's behalf, with that person's permission.

Friends, relatives and legal representatives on behalf of a dead person.

Cost

Free to complainants.

Geographical limits

The service complained of must have been provided in the Republic of Ireland.

Complainants do not have to be resident in the Republic.

Time limits

Complaints must be brought within 6 years of the event from which the problem arose. (The Ombudsman has no discretion to waive this time limit.)

Remedies

Financial compensation

Maximum IR£30,000. Typical actual awards in 1995: IR£1,000 for damages (highest was IR£20,000); IR£750 for breach of contract (highest was IR£17,000); and IR£500 to correct an error (highest was IR£5,000).

Can award interest on compensation, and require the bank or building society to pay the complainant's necessary costs of legal or expert advice.

Can reduce the amount of an award if he thinks the actions of the complainant contributed to the problem.

Other

Can recommend corrective action such as the correction of mistakes or records, or the return of documents. Can recommend making an apology.

2. The complaints procedure

Making the complaint

Complaints must be in writing. There is a standard complaint form and guidance leaflet.

Exhausting the internal complaints procedure

The complainant must have exhausted the bank or building society's internal complaints procedure before the Ombudsman can conduct a formal investigation. It is up to the Ombudsman to decide whether this has happened (no formal letter is required). If the internal complaints system has not been exhausted, the Ombudsman gives detailed instructions to the complainant about how and to whom to make the complaint. He does not give advice on the rights or wrongs of the case at this stage.

Powers of investigation

Can seek an answer to any question and see any documents he considers relevant.

Criteria for decisions

What is fair and reasonable in the circumstances, taking account of the criteria that apply in a court of law and good practice in the industry. Most emphasis is placed on what is fair and reasonable, unless outweighed by legal or statutory requirements.

The Ombudsman is not bound to follow his own previous decisions, although he does aim for consistency.

Confidentiality

During an investigation, the bank or building society concerned is sent all documentation supplied by the complainant. The complainant is supplied with copy documents sent by the institution only if the Ombudsman thinks it is necessary, for instance if there is a dispute about a signature. Documents can be submitted in confidence by either side, but will carry less weight than those that are allowed to be disclosed to the other party.

Summaries of noteworthy cases are published in the *Annual Report*, but they are anonymous: no details are given which could possibly identify the complainant or the institution.

Stages in complaint resolution

Preliminary stage

Staff will give any help needed to make the complaint. Complaints are screened by a complaints officer to check that they are within jurisdiction and the complainant receives a preliminary letter of information.

If the complaint is not 'mature' (that is, it has not exhausted the internal complaints system), the complainant is referred to the designated person in the institution in question. The complainant is advised to come back to the Ombudsman with a signed 'waiver of confidentiality' form if not satisfied with the institution's response. (99% of complaints that come directly to the office have not yet exhausted the bank's or building society's internal complaints procedure.)

Cases not within the scheme's remit are automatically forwarded to any other body which might be able to help.

Mature complaints

So long as the complaint is within the scheme's jurisdiction, a case investigator drafts a formal complaint and written questions. These are signed by the Ombudsman and sent to the bank or building society concerned, which has 6 weeks to respond.

Investigation and draft report

The case is allocated to an investigator who examines the complaint and the response. All evidence is in writing. Interviews and hearings are not held. The investigator then prepares a draft report. This is reviewed and signed by the Ombudsman and sent to both parties, giving them 30 days to make submissions.

Final report

Any submissions are considered. The Ombudsman then issues a final report and formally requests the institution to implement any remedy he has decided upon. The file is only closed when the institution concerned has notified the Ombudsman that this has happened.

Progress reports

No progress reports are sent, unless requested.

Types of ruling

Informal conciliation

Around 15% of mature cases are settled in this way.

Binding decision

The Ombudsman's decisions are only binding on the scheme member.

Rights of appeal against a decision

There is no further appeal within the scheme.

Complainants keep their right to take a case to the courts.

The scheme is probably not subject to judicial review.

The Ombudsman does not have the right to refer a case to the courts to resolve a point of law.

Failure to comply with rulings

The Ombudsman has no formal powers to enforce his decisions. The scheme's Board could sue a member who failed to comply. In practice, there have been no failures to comply.

How long does the process take?

Target timescale

105 days from formal complaint to final decision.

Actual timescale

120 days (an increase over the previous year).

The complaints procedure can be accelerated when the Ombudsman thinks it appropriate.

Delegation of decision-making

There is no Deputy Ombudsman. While the drafting of provisional decisions is delegated to case investigators, the Ombudsman reads, approves and signs every draft and final decision letter.

Following up complaints

Where a complaint results in a formal decision by the Ombudsman, the complainant is asked to verify that the decision has been complied with by the bank or building society.

Complaints that are not within the scheme's remit are not followed up.

Complaining about the scheme itself

The Ombudsman deals with complaints about the scheme's service. (Six complaints have been received; none were upheld.)

3. The scheme's structure and administration

Origins and membership

Started operating in October 1990. Set up as a company limited by guarantee and not having share capital. Membership is voluntary: all banks and building societies in the Irish Republic belong.

Structure and accountability

The scheme is overseen by a Council and a Board.

The Council

Membership

9 members - 4 industry representatives appointed by the scheme's members, 4 lay people co-opted by the Council, plus the chairman, a lay person appointed by the members.

Role

The Council appoints the Ombudsman, ensures his independence, gives him general guidance and support, approves his *Annual Report*, monitors the scheme's terms of reference and general functioning and makes appropriate recommendations to the Board. Plays no part in any aspect of the Ombudsman's decisions or investigations. Meets quarterly.

The Board

Membership

18 - all appointed by the scheme members.

Role

Decides the scheme's terms of reference; provides its funds; has a veto on the appointment and re-appointment of the Ombudsman. Plays no part in the resolution of complaints. Meets quarterly.

The Ombudsman

Appointment

By the Council. Can only be removed on bankruptcy, imprisonment of more than six months, a conviction for fraud, or becoming of unsound mind.

Term of appointment

Initially 5 years, with re-appointment permitted.

Role

Responsibility for running the office and the resolution of complaints.

Scheme's terms of reference

Set out in the document that established the scheme.

Monitoring

None at present.

BIOA member?

Yes.

Funding

Member banks and building societies pay a levy in proportion to the size of their customer base.

Costs

Running cost

IR£265,000 in 1994/95.

Cost per complaint

Not published.

Staffing

2 (legally qualified) investigators, a complaints officer and a secretary.

Forthcoming changes

None planned.

Improving best practice

The Ombudsman has no formal powers to improve best practice among credit institutions.

Facts and figures

New complaints received in writing (including ineligible complaints)

Subject of complaint	1993/94	1994/95
Lending	308	241
Operation of accounts	264	279
Mortgages	302	233
Credit cards	38	37
Investments	44	79
Service	61	89
ATMs (cash machines)	27	18
Foreign exchange	14	20
Sundry	3	4

Complaints at each stage of procedure

	1993/94	1994/95	% change
New complaints received	1,061	1,000	
Complaints sent back to internal procedure	971	919	
Complaints not within remit/referred elsewhere	90	81	
Formal complaints made	365	357	-2
Draft reports issued	305	283	-7
Final decisions issued	305	283	

Outcome of complaints fully investigated

Complaint upheld	132 (46%)	102 (39%)	-
Complaint not upheld	152 (54%)	162 (61%)	-
Complaint settled/withdrawn	21	19	-

Information available about the scheme

Publicising the scheme

Member banks and building societies have a contractual obligation under the scheme to inform their customers of the scheme's existence.

Leaflets and posters are on display in bank and building society branches (a 1995 survey showed that material was on display in over 80% of branches).

The Ombudsman responds to media questions.

Terms of reference

Published in the *Annual Report* and sent out on request.

Annual Report

Usually published in November. Includes analyses of the causes of complaints, historical complaints statistics, and breakdowns of complaints by types of institution. Information relating to limited companies is included.

Broadcasting Standards Commission

7 The Sanctuary, London SW1P 3JS
Tel: 0171 233 0544. Fax: 0171 233 0397

Chair: The Lady Howe
Deputy Chair: Jane Leighton

On 1 April 1997 the Broadcasting Complaints Commission merged with the Broadcasting Standards Council to become the Broadcasting Standards Commission. Within the Commission there are separate committees dealing with complaints about standards and complaints about fairness and privacy. This entry deals with complaints about fairness and privacy only.

Chair: Fairness and Privacy Committee: Jane Leighton

1. Using the scheme: key points

Service-providers covered

All sound and television broadcasters.

Complaints covered

Complaints of unfair or unjust treatment in programmes.

Complaints of unwarranted infringement of privacy in programmes, or in connection with the obtaining of material included in programmes.

Complaints not covered

Complaints concerning the portrayal of sex and violence.

Complaints relating to a programme broadcast more than 5 years after the death of the person affected.

Complaints about scheduling.

Frivolous complaints.

Cases already subject to court proceedings.

Other complaints can be turned away if the Commission considers them inappropriate for any reason.

Who can complain?

Individuals, groups of people, businesses, partnerships, charities and other incorporated bodies.

Personal representatives, relatives or other closely connected people can, if properly authorised, complain on behalf of an individual who cannot complain himself or herself (because of death or some other reason).

Cost

None to complainants.

Complainants who choose to be legally represented will not be able to recover those costs from the scheme.

Geographical limits

Complainants do not have to be resident in the UK and it does not matter in which country the complaint arose.

The offending programme must have been broadcast by a UK licence-holder.

Time limits

There is no fixed period within which complaints must be brought - but the Commission usually turns away complaints made after 3 months (for television broadcasts) and 6 weeks (for radio broadcasts). For complaints outside these time limits, the Commission exercises its discretion, taking account of any special individual circumstances.

Remedies

Financial compensation

None. The Commission cannot require broadcasters to pay financial compensation. Costs cannot be awarded to either party.

Other

Broadcast and publication of a summary of the Commission's findings.

The Commission can require the broadcasters to broadcast the summary of the adjudication on the same channel and at a similar time to the programme complained about. It can also require the broadcaster to publish the summary in appropriate publications.

The Commission cannot require broadcasters to apologise to the complainant or broadcast a correction.

2. The complaints procedure

Making the complaint

Complainants can complain to the Commission direct. Complaints must be in writing on a standard form: a guidance leaflet is available.

Exhausting the internal complaints procedure

Complainants do not have to exhaust broadcasters' internal channels of complaint before the Commission will investigate.

Powers of investigation

The broadcaster concerned must, by law, provide a written statement, recordings, transcripts of the programme, and copies of any correspondence with the person affected or the complainant.

Can require broadcasters to attend a hearing.

Criteria for decisions

Commission members decide cases by majority vote, having established as far as possible all the relevant facts.

Each case is dealt with strictly on its own merits but the Commissioners aim to act consistently, taking account of experience and decisions in earlier cases.

Confidentiality

During the investigation, all correspondence and written submissions from each side are copied to the other. When a complaint is upheld, details are usually broadcast and published in summary form. Whether or not a complaint is upheld, details are published in the Commission's monthly Bulletin and full adjudications are available on request to any interested party.

The name of the complainant is usually published, unless there is a good reason for not disclosing it. The names of the broadcaster and the programme are always published.

Stages in complaint resolution

Preliminary stage

The Commission decides whether to consider the complaint. If it is clearly outside the scheme's remit (for instance, if it concerns scheduling), the complainant is sent a letter of explanation.

If it is within the remit of another broadcasting authority, the complaint will be forwarded automatically. If it concerns taste, decency and the like, it will be considered by another appropriate panel of the Broadcasting Standards Commission or the appropriate regulatory body (BBC governors, Independent Television Commission or Welsh Authority).

Investigation and hearing

If the Commission decides to handle the complaint, a copy goes to the broadcasters, requiring them to provide (usually within 4 weeks) a video cassette or tape and transcript of the programme, any related correspondence, and a written statement in answer. A copy of the complaint is also sent to the regulatory body, the BBC or the Welsh Authority, as appropriate.

Once the broadcaster's statement has been received, the Commission will give the complainant the opportunity to respond, in writing, direct to the Commission (normally within 2 weeks). The response is sent to the broadcaster who can make a further written statement if it wishes (within 2 weeks).

Usually no more written comments are accepted from either side and in the majority of cases the Commission arranges a hearing in private at its office to enable Commissioners to ask questions about conflicts of facts as seen by either side. The complainant, any key witnesses and representatives of the broadcasters are invited.

Adjudication

The Commission then reaches its findings, which are set out in a written adjudication. (Neither complainants nor broadcasters see draft adjudications, although in the event of the complaint being upheld both are invited to comment on a summary of the Commission's findings prepared for publication.) Copies of the adjudication and, where relevant, of the summary are sent to the complainant and the broadcasters at the same time.

Where the complaint has been upheld, the Commission usually directs the broadcasters to broadcast the summary of the adjudication and to publish it in the Radio Times or other appropriate publications. The summary is usually broadcast on the same channel and at a similar time as the programme that was the subject of the complaint.

Progress reports

Letters are sent as each stage of the complaints procedure is reached.

Types of ruling

Informal conciliation

Less than 5% of complaints are resolved in this way.

Formal adjudication

This is binding on both parties (95% or more of complaints are dealt with in this way).

Rights of appeal against a decision

Neither party can require the Commission to reconsider its final decision and there is no appeal to an external body. (Complaints about the Commission's procedures can however be made to the Chair.)

The scheme is subject to judicial review. (There have been 9 judicial reviews over the lifetime of the former Broadcasting Complaints Commission.)

Failure to comply with rulings

The only sanction is for the Commission to direct the broadcast and publication of a summary of its findings - which it normally does in any case whenever a complaint is upheld. (There has been non-compliance in less than 1% of cases.) The Commission can also write to broadcasting regulators - the Independent Television Commission or the Radio Authority.

How long does the process take?

Up to 11 months from the time a complaint is first accepted to adjudication. (During 1997 the Commission intends to clear the current backlog and, from April 1998, to reduce the time to 5 months.)

Delegation of decision-making

The fairness director to the scheme, in consultation with the legal adviser, makes an initial decision on whether complaints are within the scheme's jurisdiction. The Commission members who have considered the case read through and sign all final adjudications.

Following up complaints

If the Commission cannot deal with a complaint it is not followed up.

The Commission checks that its directions to publish findings have been carried out.

Complaining about the scheme itself

> Complaints about the Commission's procedures can be made to the Chair.

3. The scheme's structure and administration

Origins and membership

> Started operating in 1981, was later re-established under the Broadcasting Act 1990 as the Broadcasting Complaints Commission. On 1 April 1997, under the Broadcasting Act 1996, the Broadcasting Complaints Commission and the Broadcasting Standards Council were merged to become the Broadcasting Standards Commission.

Structure and accountability

> The Broadcasting Standards Commission is accountable to the Department of National Heritage and the Secretary of State oversees its activities. There is no exact equivalent of an Ombudsman.

Membership

> Usually 11 commissioners, including the chair, all appointed by the Secretary of State for National Heritage, under the Broadcasting Act 1996. Anyone with a current connection with the broadcasters covered by the scheme or their regulatory bodies, or any other current interest in providing programmes for them, is disqualified. The Act makes no provision for dismissal.

Term of appointment

> Usually 3 years.

Role

> To consider complaints covered by the scheme. Commissioners also decide whether a complainant's interest in the subject matter of the complaint is sufficiently direct and that they are the person(s) affected by the programme.

Scheme's terms of reference

These are laid down by statute and could only be changed by amending legislation.

Monitoring

Standards of service and performance indicators are published in the *Annual Report*.

BIOA member?

Yes.

Funding

Provided by the Department of National Heritage which recoups half of the cost of the full Commission from broadcasters in proportion to the number of complaints received.

Costs

Running cost

£608,835 in 1996/97 (£556,602 in 1995/96).

Cost per complaint

Not available.

Staffing

Day-to-day management of the office is the director's responsibility. Supporting the commissioners in handling both fairness and privacy complaints and complaints about standards of taste and decency are the director, the deputy director, the fairness director, the communications director and deputy director, the research director and deputy director, three part-time legal advisers, 7 case managers, a part-time accountant and 10 administrative staff.

Forthcoming changes

The Commission became a new body from 1 April 1997.

Improving best practice

The Commission has no powers beyond recommending improvements through its *Annual Report*.

Facts and figures

Numbers of complaints determined

Subject of complaint	1995/96	1996/97	% change
Unjust or unfair treatment - television	32	33	3
Unjust or unfair treatment - radio	4	10	150
Unwarranted infringement of privacy - television	6	9	50
Unwarranted infringement of privacy - radio	0	0	-
Both categories - television	17	16	-6
Both categories - radio	2	3	50

[1] Numbers too small for percentages to be significant.

Numbers of complaints at each stage of procedure

	1995/96	1996/97	% change
Total complaints handled	1,093	990	-9
Complaints not within remit/sent elsewhere	926	865	-7
Complaints adjudicated upon	61	74 [1]	21

Outcome

Complaint upheld	17 (28%)	27 (38%)[1]
Complaint upheld in part	22 (36%)	15 (21%)[1]
Complaint dismissed	22 (36%)	29 (41%)[1]

[1] 74 complaints resulted in 71 adjudications.

Information available about the scheme

Publicising the scheme

Broadcasters must, by law, broadcast regular announcements publicising the Commission.

There is a scheme leaflet for the public and guidance notes for organisations covered by the scheme.

Annual Report

Usually published in July. Includes historic information on the number of complaints, accounts, breakdown of complaints by type of complainant (whether an individual or company for instance), programme type and programme channel. All complaints are listed.

Other publications

The Commission's adjudications are made widely available and details are included in the Commission's monthly Bulletin.

The full text of all the year's adjudications are available in hard copy for £10 and free on disk.

Ombudsman for Corporate Estate Agents

Beckett House, 4 Bridge Street, Salisbury, Wiltshire SP1 2LX
Tel: 01722 333306. Fax: 01722 332296

Ombudsman: David Quayle

1. Using the scheme: key points

Service-providers covered

Large corporate estate agents. Any business that is, or is a subsidiary of, a bank, building society or company listed on the Stock Exchange, and which carries on estate agency work, is eligible to join the scheme. About half of eligible estate agencies are members.

Complaints covered

Complaints that the estate agency has infringed the complainant's legal rights, treated him or her unfairly or been guilty of maladministration (including inefficiency or undue delay), in a way that results in financial loss or inconvenience.

Complaints not covered

Commercial decisions.

Disputes over a survey.

Disputes concerning the letting of residential property.

Complaints concerning commercial and agricultural property.

Complaints about services provided on special terms to an employee of a member agency or his/her spouse or partner.

Complaints involving claims of more than £100,000.

Usually, cases on which a court has already ruled or which are already subject to court proceedings. However:

- members keep the right to take legal action to enforce the payment of their commission following a sale, even when they are aware that the defendant intends to take a complaint to the Ombudsman;

- complainants also retain the right to settle the bill 'without prejudice', which would then allow the Ombudsman to review a complaint;

- where the complainant does not settle a bill before taking a complaint to the Ombudsman and a court rules that the agency is entitled to payment, the agency has the right not to permit the Ombudsman to review any other elements of the case until payment is received. (In practice, a member agency has only once exercised this right.)

Who can complain?

Individuals and groups of individuals who are actual or potential buyers or sellers of residential property through a member estate agency. Not bodies such as businesses or charities.

A third party on behalf of a living individual.

The personal representatives or beneficiaries of a dead person.

Cost

Free to complainants.

Geographical limits

Complaints arising only in the United Kingdom (excluding the Channel Islands and Isle Of Man).

There is no restriction on the complainant's place of residence.

Time limits

Complaints must be referred to the estate agency itself within 12 months of the event from which the complaint arose.

The complaint must be referred to the Ombudsman within 6 months of the complainant receiving notice of the agency's final position.

The Ombudsman can investigate complaints outside these time limits when requested, or agreed to, by the agency.

Remedies

Financial compensation

A financial award is the only remedy.

Awards may be made for actual financial loss, or inconvenience or stress up to a maximum of £100,000 for each. Typical actual awards are £40 to £1,000 for financial loss (highest actual award £13,000) and £100 to £500 for inconvenience/ stress (highest actual award £1,000).

The Ombudsman does not directly order payment of interest on awards, but considers the time taken to reach a resolution when assessing the value of an award.

An award may be reduced if, in the Ombudsman's opinion, the complainant's actions contributed to the problem.

The Ombudsman can award the costs of legal or other expert advice against the member agency (though this seldom happens in practice).

2. The complaints procedure

Making the complaint

Complainants can approach the scheme direct or through an intermediary, such as an MP. Complaints must be in writing (telephoned complaints must be followed by written confirmation). There is no standard complaints form, but the scheme issues a *Consumer Guide* and guidance letters. Those with difficulty making a complaint are also given help over the telephone or referred to a citizens advice bureau.

Exhausting the internal complaints procedure

Complainants must first exhaust the estate agent's own internal channels of complaint: the complainant needs a specific letter from the agency stating the agency's final position. If all internal channels of complaint have not been exhausted, the scheme may advise the complainant on how best to take the complaint forward and the options open if threatened with legal action, for example, for non payment of the agent's fees. (See also Stages in complaint resolution below.)

Powers of investigation

The Ombudsman can demand the production of papers by member estate agencies, if they do not provide them voluntarily (as they always have done so far).

Criteria for decisions

The Ombudsman scheme's code of practice and what is fair and reasonable.

Each case is treated on its individual merits, taking previous decisions into account as far as is sensible.

Confidentiality

No documentation sent to the Ombudsman by one party is copied to the other.

The Ombudsman publishes anonymous details of noteworthy cases in the *Annual Report*. The names of complainants and member agencies are not published.

Stages in complaint resolution

Initial enquiries

Around 90% of initial enquiries concern complaints where the estate agency's internal complaints procedure has not yet been exhausted. In this instance, a case processing officer advises the complainant how to pursue the complaint. During an internal complaints procedure, complainants sometimes ask the Ombudsman whether he considers an offer made by a member agency to be fair. Where he feels the offer is not unreasonable, he will tell the complainant so; if he thinks it is on the low side, he will contact the member agency to seek an improved offer which he will then put forward to the complainant. The decision whether or not to accept remains with the complainant.

If a complaint is not within scheme's remit, staff will advise on the alternatives - for instance, a local citizens advice bureau, a professional body or trade association, or another ombudsman scheme or regulatory body.

Investigation and assessment

If an eligible complaint remains unresolved, the complainant is asked to sign a 'waiver of confidentiality' form, authorising the member agency to release its files to the Ombudsman. Further information may also be requested from the complainant, member agency or any other parties involved. Either the Ombudsman or the case officer now assesses the case.

If the evidence does not bear out the complaint, the complainant is sent a letter stating that, unless new evidence comes to light, it would be unfruitful to pursue the claim through the scheme. The complainant has 4 weeks (extended on request) to put forward any further points. Interviews and hearings are possible (at the Ombudsman's office) but very rare: the telephone is used extensively.

Decision and recommendation

For complaints that are found to be justified, the Ombudsman first looks to see whether any compensation was offered during the internal complaints procedure. If it was, that offer (or a higher one if it has been negotiated) can be revived for a set period. The Ombudsman then writes to the complainant explaining why he believes the offer to be fair.

In the majority of cases where the Ombudsman finds for the complainant, a more formal procedure is adopted. The Ombudsman drafts a proposed recommendation and award and sends it to the member agency (which has 4 weeks to comment on it), and then the complainant (who has 2 weeks to comment). The complainant and/or the agency can have longer, on request. The Ombudsman then issues a final recommendation and award. The member agency has 2 weeks to implement it.

Progress reports

Complainants are informed by monthly letter if the complaint is taking longer than usual to settle.

Types of ruling

Mediation

In 1996 14% of complaints were settled following the scheme's mediation.

A decision by the Ombudsman

This is binding on the member agency but not on the complainant. A few cases which are investigated do not proceed to a decision (1.5% in 1996), either because they are thought to be more suitable for resolution in court or because they are found to be outside the terms of reference.

Rights of appeal against a decision

Complainants have no right of appeal against the Ombudsman's decision, but they do retain the right to take their case to court.

Decisions are binding on member agencies and they have no right of appeal.

It has not been established whether the scheme is subject to judicial review.

Failure to comply with rulings

There have been no cases of non-compliance. A member could be expelled from the scheme.

How long does the process take?

Target timescale

> 1 month to start the formal review of a complaint after receiving the member agency's file.

Actual timescale

> Over 98% of cases are completed within 3 months of receiving the file.

Delegation of decision-making

> There is no Deputy Ombudsman. The Ombudsman's powers to decide on complaints are not delegated in any way.

Following up complaints

> The Ombudsman usually requires written confirmation from the member agency that the decision has been complied with.

Complaining about the scheme itself

> The Ombudsman brings complaints about the scheme to the attention of the chairman of the Council. (There has been one complaint in the scheme's lifetime: it was not upheld.)

3. The scheme's structure and administration

Origins and membership

> Started operating on 12 September 1990. Set up as a company limited by guarantee.

> It is a voluntary scheme, with a code of practice which members are expected to observe. Currently 50% of eligible institutions are members (a number left during the contraction in the housing market). Non-members are usually small independent firms.

Structure and accountability

The scheme is accountable to the Council of the Ombudsman of Corporate Estate Agents (OCEA) and to the Board of OCEA Company Ltd.

The Council

Membership

7 members: 2 are industry representatives appointed by the Board (subject to approval by the Council). 5 (including the chairman) are lay members. The chairman is appointed by the Board (with Council approval); the lay members are co-opted. Approval of appointments cannot unreasonably be withheld by the Board or the Council.

Role

To appoint the Ombudsman (subject to Board approval) and protect his independence; to approve his *Annual Report* and draft budget; to recommend to the Board any changes to the terms of reference it thinks necessary. Plays no part in the resolution of individual complaints, can (and does) give general guidance to the Ombudsman. Meets quarterly.

The Board

Membership

Currently 6 directors from the member agencies, and an independent chairman appointed by the Board.

Role

To approve the annual budget; to levy the necessary funds from member agencies; to authorise any changes to the terms of reference and code of practice. Plays no part in the resolution of individual complaints. Meets quarterly.

The Ombudsman

Appointment

By the Council. Can be dismissed on becoming bankrupt or of unsound mind, or for any act which, in the opinion of the Board, is likely to lead himself or the scheme into disrepute.

Term of appointment

2-year periods, may be reappointed.

Role

The Ombudsman has overall responsibility for running the office and complaints-handling.

Scheme's terms of reference

These are set out in the document establishing the scheme. They can be changed, taking into account recommendations by the Council.

Monitoring

No routine monitoring.

BIOA member?

Yes.

Funding

Member estate agencies fund the scheme. They pay a flat fee based on the number of agency offices each has open on 31 July each year.

Costs

Running cost

£230,522 in 1995 (this figure is falling).

Cost per complaint

Not published.

Staffing

The Ombudsman's assistant acts as the office manager. In addition, there is 1 part-time case officer (legally qualified), 1 full-time case processing officer (with estate agency and building society experience), a part-time case processing officer and a part-time secretary.

Forthcoming changes

Discussions continue with the Royal Institution of Chartered Surveyors, National Association of Estate Agents, Incorporated Society of Valuers and Auctioneers and the Office of Fair Trading, with the aim of issuing a joint code of practice and establishing a new Ombudsman scheme open to members of these professional bodies.

Improving best practice

The Ombudsman may (and in practice does) recommend changes to the procedures of individual member agencies or amendments to the scheme's code of practice (through the Council and Board).

Facts and figures

Numbers of new complaints received in writing (including ineligible complaints and telephone enquiries)[1]

Subject of complaint	1995	1996	% change
Maladministration	391	573	[2]
Commission/fees	200	293	[2]
Communication of other offers to the buyer	200	255	[2]
Sales particulars	138	133	[2]
Communication of offers to the seller	85	117	[2]
Gazumping	45	93	[2]
Viewing and keys	36	63	[2]
Initial valuation for sale	32	42	[2]
Buyer's finances	23	33	[2]
Conflict of interests	12	3	[2]
Unfair bias towards other party	9	19	[2]
Sale boards	8	13	[2]
Sealed bids	4	-	[2]
Offer of financial services	1	-	[2]

[1] Where it is possible to identify more than one main element within an individual complaint, both are included in the statistics above.
[2] Percentage changes are not significant because of the reduction in membership over this period.

Numbers of complaints at each stage of procedure

	1995	1996	% change
Initial enquiries containing at least an element of dissatisfaction with the performance of an estate agent	2,483	2,705	[1]
Complaints outside terms of reference as concerning non-member agencies	1,364	1,506	[1]
Complaints outside terms of reference for other reason/not disclosed	317	318	[1]
Cases closed	229	266	[1]
Cases closed following negotiated settlements	31	32	[1]
Cases found during investigation to be outside terms of reference	4	4	[1]

[1] Percentage changes are not significant because of the reduction in membership over this period.

Outcome of formal decisions

	1995	**1996**	**% change**
Favourable to complainant	79 (41%)	84 (37%)	[1]
Favourable to member agency	115 (59%)	146 (63%)	[1]

[1] Percentage changes are not significant because of the reduction in membership over this period.

Information available about the scheme

Publicising the scheme

Member agencies must display the scheme logo on all advertising material and stationery. They are also encouraged to mention the scheme to all prospective buyers and sellers, to display a notice in their offices and to distribute the scheme leaflet.

The *Consumer Guide* leaflet is available in all members' agencies.

Terms of reference

Published and available on request.

Annual Report

In addition to the tables above this includes a breakdown of cases formally reviewed by nature of complaint.

Other publications

Rhoda James, 'The Ombudsman for corporate estate agents - putting half the house in order', *Consumer Law Journal*, vol. 3, issue 5, 1995.

P.E. Morris, 'The Ombudsman for corporate estate agents', *Civil Justice Quarterly*, October 1994.

The scheme also publishes a Code of Practice (in 2 versions - one for Scotland, one for England, Wales and Northern Ireland).

Funeral Ombudsman

26-28 Bedford Row, London WC1R 4HE
Tel: 0171 430 1112. Fax: 0171 430 1012

Ombudsman: Professor Geoffrey Woodroffe

1. Using the scheme: key points

Service-providers covered

Funeral directors who are members of the Funeral Standards Council.

Funeral planning companies which are members of the Funeral Planning Council.

Funeral directors who join the scheme independently.

Almost half the industry are members.

Complaints covered

Complaints about any aspect of the service provided, including the marketing, management and administration of funerals and funeral planning services.

Providing the funeral company member agrees, a complaint about any other matter in connection with funerals for which there is no other Ombudsman with equivalent powers.

Complaints not covered

Complaints involving claims of more than £100,000.

Complaints about services provided to someone by virtue of the fact that he or she (or the spouse) is or was an employee of the funeral company.

Complaints about matters that took place before 4 April 1994.

Complaints about any service provided by the funeral company in its capacity as an authorised investment business under the Financial Services Act (for which there are alternative Ombudsman schemes).

Complaints that have been, or become, the subject of proceedings before any court, arbitrator or other independent conciliation body. The Ombudsman can also decide not to investigate a complaint, or to stop an investigation, if he thinks it would be more appropriately dealt with by a court, arbitrator or other independent complaints-handling scheme.

Who can complain?

The individual who employed the services of the funeral company, or someone else on their behalf.

Personal representatives of an individual customer.

Cost

Free to complainants.

Geographical limits

None.

Time limits

The complaint must be made

- no more than 2 years after the event which led to the complaint, and

- no more than 6 months after the later of: the date when the complainant received the funeral company's final response to the complaint; or the date when the complainant was notified of the right to take a complaint to the Ombudsman.

The Ombudsman can decide to waive these time limits if it was not reasonably practical for the complaint to be made earlier and/or there are extenuating circumstances.

Remedies

Financial compensation

Maximum compensation: £50,000, which can include up to £5,000 for distress and inconvenience. (Average actual award: £900. Highest actual award in the scheme's lifetime: £2,665.) The complainant remains responsible for the balance of any payment due to the service provider.

Can order the payment of interest on an award.

Can award the complainant the costs of legal or other expert advice.

May reduce the amount of an award if the complainant contributed to the problem.

Other

Can make recommendation to a member to improve its practices (for example, to use registered - rather than normal - mail for the transport of ashes).

2. The complaints procedure

Making the complaint

Complainants can approach the scheme direct or through an intermediary.

Complaints must be in writing. Telephoned complaints are acceptable to start the process off, but must be followed by written confirmation. There is no standard complaint form, but the scheme offers a guidance leaflet (with a tear-off complaint slip) and an information pack.

Exhausting the internal complaints procedure

Before the Ombudsman starts a formal investigation, complainants must first go through the funeral company's internal complaints procedure. However, the scheme gives help during this process to both the complainant and the scheme member, in the form of conciliation. When the internal complaints procedure has been exhausted, the funeral company must send a form confirming this to the Ombudsman. The Ombudsman can decide to investigate without this form, if he thinks there is good reason to do so.

Powers of investigation

Can compel the complainant and the scheme member to provide information (and can only proceed with a complaint if both parties provide the necessary information).

Cannot compel other organisations or individuals to provide papers or reports.

Criteria for decisions

The law and any relevant codes of practice.

What is fair and reasonable (in practice, the Ombudsman puts most emphasis on what is reasonable).

The Ombudsman is not bound in any way by previous decisions, although he does take them into consideration to help achieve consistency in the levels of awards.

Confidentiality

The majority of cases involve one person's word against another's: in these circumstances, each party is told what the other has claimed.

When there is written material, each party is given all the details, sometimes through a summary and sometimes through photocopies, as appropriate.

The Ombudsman publishes anonymous details of his decisions. (A full adjudication was included in the first *Annual Report*.) Any identifiable references are removed, although the Ombudsman has the power to name the funeral service member (with the complainant's permission).

Stages in complaint resolution

Preliminary stage

When a complaint is received about a funeral director who is a member of the scheme, it is acknowledged. The complainant is advised to write to a senior manager in the funeral company, if he or she has not already done so, and to send the Ombudsman copies of any correspondence received. The scheme informs the funeral company that a complaint has been received and asks for details of its own complaints procedure. For complaints that are outside the scheme's remit, every effort is made to find another suitable organisation to help: complaints can be referred - with the complainant's consent - to trade associations (if the company is a member), to various other bodies (such as associations for memorial masons, crematoria and cemeteries) and sometimes to the Local Government Ombudsman.

Conciliation

For eligible complaints, a process of conciliation begins. If telephone conversations and letters are ineffective, the solution sometimes lies in bringing the parties together in the scheme's office (or elsewhere, if more convenient).

Investigation

It is only when negotiations have failed and internal complaints procedures have been exhausted that an investigation begins. At this point both parties and any outside organisations that have been involved are asked for written statements of events surrounding the complaint. Other funeral directors and their associations may be asked for advice on the normal practices of the profession. Only in exceptional cases is there an oral hearing. The Ombudsman considers all the evidence.

Adjudication

In all cases investigated, the Ombudsman will notify both parties of his decision and give his reasons in writing: draft reports are not sent to either party for comment beforehand.

Progress reports

Complainants are kept up to date on a monthly basis.

They are informed when a complaint reaches the stage where there is to be an adjudication, and told they will get the decision in writing.

Types of ruling

Informal conciliation

Just over 90% of cases are settled in this way.

Adjudication

Investigations are followed by a decision - which is binding on the scheme member. (Fewer than 10% of cases are formally investigated.)

Rights of appeal against a decision

The complainant keeps the right to take legal action against the member if dissatisfied with the Ombudsman's decision (no one has yet done so in practice).

Funeral company members have no right of appeal against a decision.

The scheme is unlikely to be subject to judicial review.

Failure to comply with rulings

If a member fails to comply, the Ombudsman will report the company to the relevant professional association. He also has the power to publish details of the non-compliance, for example by including the name of the member and details of the case in the *Annual Report* (so long as the complainant agrees). (In practice no member has failed to comply with a decision.)

How long does the process take?

Timescales vary, but usually 8 to 12 weeks, (unless there is an adjudication).

Delegation of decision-making

There is no Deputy Ombudsman. The Ombudsman's powers to decide on a complaint are not delegated.

Following up complaints

> After an investigation, the Ombudsman writes to the funeral company to check that the decision has been complied with.

Complaining about the scheme itself

> No set procedure (as the scheme is still too small).

3. The scheme's structure and administration

Origins and membership

> A voluntary scheme set up as a company limited by guarantee.
>
> Started operating on 4 April 1994.

Structure and accountability

> The scheme is overseen by a Council and a Board.

The Council

Membership

> Currently 7: 2 industry and 5 lay representatives. Majority of Council members must be independent of the industry, and at least 3 must be consumer representatives. The chairman is a lay member. Meets about 5 times a year.

Role

> To appoint the Ombudsman; to define his powers and terms of reference; to approve his *Annual Report* and the budget. Plays no part in how complaints are dealt with.

The Board

Membership

> 3, all industry representatives. The Board meets once a year.

Role

> Various powers given by the company articles (for instance, to determine the budget and raise funds from members). Plays no part in the resolution of complaints.

The Ombudsman

Appointment

> By the Council. May be dismissed on grounds of bankruptcy, insanity and the usual employment grounds (like misconduct).

Term of appointment

> Initially 3 years, renewable in 3-yearly terms.

Role

> Responsibility for running the office and complaints-handling.

Scheme's terms of reference

> These are set down in the document establishing the scheme. Can be changed by amending the company memorandum and articles.

Monitoring

> No routine monitoring.

BIOA member?

> Yes.

Funding

> Funding comes from the Funeral Standards Council and the Funeral Planning Council.

Costs

Running cost

> £120,000 in 1996 (no change over previous year).

Cost per complaint

> Not published.

Staffing

Overall responsibility

The Ombudsman.

Staff

2 - the scheme administrator and an administrative assistant.

Forthcoming changes

The Ombudsman hopes the scheme will gain new members and more support from other funeral associations.

Improving best practice

The Ombudsman can make recommendations to the industry in adjudications or in his *Annual Report*.

Facts and figures

Numbers of complaints at each stage of procedure

	21 months to 31/12/95	12 months to 31/12/96	% change
Total complaints handled	96	81	[1]
Complaints not within remit/referred elsewhere	50	48	[1]
Formal adjudications	5	8	[1]
Outcome of complaints fully investigated			
Complaint not upheld	1 (20%)	0	-
Complaint upheld/upheld in part	4 (80%)	6 (100%)	-

[1] Not significant as periods are of different lengths.

Information available about the scheme

Publicising the scheme

Members are obliged, under their codes of practice, to inform their customers of the existence of the scheme.

An information pack and consumer leaflet is distributed to consumer organisations.

Publishes articles in the trade and consumer press. Has held receptions and press conferences in Northern Ireland, Scotland and Wales.

Terms of reference

Published in the scheme's first *Annual Report* (1994/95).

Annual Report

Published in April. In addition to the table above, the *Annual Report* gives more information about complaints that fall outside the scheme's remit.

Parliamentary Ombudsman

(The Parliamentary Commissioner for Administration)

Church House, Great Smith Street, London SW1P 3BW
Tel: 0171 276 2130/3000. Fax: 0171 276 2135

Ombudsman: Michael Buckley

This Ombudsman also holds the post of Health Service Ombudsman.

1. Using the scheme: key points

Service-providers covered

Government departments, their executive agencies and around 50 non-departmental public bodies (there is a full list in the scheme's leaflet).

Administrative staff appointed by the Lord Chancellor to work for courts or tribunals.

Administrative staff of other tribunals appointed by other government ministers (for example, those in the Independent Tribunals Service).

Some of the UK government's consular functions.

Complaints covered

Complaints that maladministration (administrative failure) has led to injustice. These can include:

- complaints that official information has been unreasonably misused;

- complaints about actions carried out on behalf of an organisation covered by the scheme - for example, where a private contractor performs functions previously carried out by a government department.

Complaints not covered

Complaints concerning government policy or the content of legislation.

Complaints about matters affecting relations with other governments or with international organisations, or the actions of government employees overseas - unless they concern consular functions.

Complaints about the investigation of crime or the protection of national security (although other Ombudsmen cover some of these areas - see separate section on Police page 285).

Complaints concerning the commencement or conduct of court proceedings (but the administrative actions of court staff are covered, except in Scotland).

Complaints concerning the contractual or other commercial dealings of bodies covered by the scheme, except the compulsory purchase of land or its subsequent disposal.

Complaints concerning public service personnel matters.

Usually, complaints for which there are other ways of obtaining a remedy - for example, a right of appeal to an independent tribunal or a right to take a case to the courts. However, the Ombudsman may in some circumstances decide to investigate if the complainant has not used those other rights.

Who can complain?

All complaints must be referred to the Ombudsman by an MP.

Individuals, groups of individuals, corporate bodies, partnerships, charities etc. whose complaint arose from events that occurred in the UK, or if a resident, when using one of the consular services covered by the scheme abroad.

Legal representatives or others on an individual's behalf.

Personal representatives on behalf of a dead person.

Complaints cannot be made by a local authority, nationalised industry, or any authority whose members are appointed by the Crown or by ministers, or whose revenues are wholly or mainly provided by parliament.

Cost

Free to complainants.

Geographical limits

A complaint may be put:

- by any individual citizen of the UK;

- by any foreign national complaining about an action taken while he or she was in the UK;

- about an action taken in the UK or abroad in the exercise of consular function on behalf of the UK government.

Time limits

Usually, the Ombudsman cannot investigate complaints about events which took place more than 12 months before the complainant first contacted his or her MP. However, the Ombudsman can decide to waive this time limit in exceptional cases.

Remedies

Financial compensation

Can recommend payment of compensation to the complainant and to any others who have suffered in the same way (the Treasury issues guidance on redress and compensation: reference DAO(GEN) 15/92).

Other

Can recommend that appropriate procedures should be put in place or, if already in place, that they should be properly observed or clarified.

2. The complaints procedure

Making the complaint

Complaints must be referred by an MP (usually the complainant's own MP), and the Ombudsman deals with the complainant through the MP. It is up to the MP to decide whether to refer a case to the Ombudsman - he or she may first ask the public body concerned to put the matter right. Complaints must be in writing. There is a complaint form in the scheme's leaflet but it is not necessary to use it. The Ombudsman's office will help if the complainant or the MP has difficulty. (Usually, the complainant provides the information and the MP passes it on to the Ombudsman.)

Exhausting the internal complaints procedure

Before an MP refers a complaint to the Ombudsman, the complainant must first pursue the matter through the organisation's own complaints procedure.

Powers of investigation

Has the power to compel witnesses to attend and answer questions, and to call for the production of documents (except information or documents relating to the proceedings of the Cabinet). Organisations covered by the scheme cannot withhold papers on the grounds of a statutory duty of confidentiality, public interest immunity or legal privilege. These powers only operate after the Ombudsman has decided to investigate a case.

Criteria for decisions

The Ombudsman applies the standard of proof that applies to civil cases in court - that is, he reaches his decisions on the balance of probabilities.

Confidentiality

Investigations are confidential. No papers are passed to the other party.

Names of complainants are not published. The name of the organisation concerned in each case is published in the *Annual Report*.

Stages in complaint resolution

Screening

New complaints are screened to establish whether they are within jurisdiction. This may reveal the need for additional information, and occasionally the screening staff may contact the organisation informally to check out the background to a complaint.

Cases not within the scheme's remit are referred to any appropriate alternative body.

Statement of complaint

Where a full investigation is to be pursued, the Ombudsman must give the principal officer or chief executive of the organisation in question an opportunity to comment. A statement of complaint is drawn up by the Ombudsman's office and sent for comment, with a copy to the complainant. Organisations are expected to give their initial comments within 3 weeks (and the select committee to which the Ombudsman is accountable has asked him to report on any cases where departments fail to provide comments within 6 weeks).

Investigation

After receiving the organisation's initial reply, the investigating officer will ask for the relevant files and, perhaps, further information from officials (including, where necessary, government ministers) and from the complainant. Interviews may be held. Sometimes staff seek evidence from other organisations not within the Ombudsman's jurisdiction (for example, the Crown Prosecution Service).

Draft report

Following the investigation, a draft report is produced setting out the evidence and, in most cases, provisional findings and a conclusion. This is sent to the relevant principal officer or chief executive of the organisation to check the accuracy of the facts and for comments on their presentation and - if the Ombudsman has found injustice as a result of maladministration - to find out whether the department is prepared to provide an appropriate remedy. The draft report is not sent to the complainant or MP.

Final report

After any changes have been made in the light of comments received, a final report is sent to the organisation concerned and to the MP (with a copy for the complainant).

Progress reports

Progress letters are sent to the MP at regular intervals.

Types of ruling

Non-binding recommendation

In cases where the Ombudsman does issue a report, he may only recommend that the department pursues a particular course of action. The majority of cases received (around 80% in 1995) are not accepted for investigation. This is not necessarily an outright rejection: it may be because the case is settled to the complainant's satisfaction at the screening stage or because the complainant has not exhausted the internal complaints procedures.

Rights of appeal against a decision

There is no appeal against a decision not to investigate a complaint. The Ombudsman has a discretion in deciding whether to begin, continue or stop an investigation. An investigation cannot be reopened after a report has been issued - but the Ombudsman can decide to open a new investigation if significant new evidence becomes available.

The Ombudsman cannot currently refer cases to the courts (but see Forthcoming changes below).

The Ombudsman's decisions are subject to judicial review. There have only ever been three judicial reviews, one successful.

Failure to comply with rulings

If the recommendations in the Ombudsman's final report are not accepted by the organisation, the Ombudsman may make a special report to parliament, and the organisation may have to appear before the select committee on the Parliamentary Commissioner for Administration. This virtually never happens - parliamentary pressure and opinion are usually an adequate incentive for organisations to comply.

How long does the process take?

Target timescale

The target for screening complaints is that 90% are dealt with within 6 weeks. Complaints about access to government information are to be resolved within 13 weeks. The target timescales for a full investigation are not published.

Actual timescale

For a full investigation - 93 weeks. For complaints about access to government information - 45 weeks.

Current screening time can be significantly longer than 6 weeks but remedial action has been taken which should remedy this in most cases.

Sometimes the initial contact from the Ombudsman's office prompts departments to look afresh at a complaint and remedy it immediately (without prejudice to the outcome of any Ombudsman's investigation). In these cases, under a fast-track procedure, the Ombudsman immediately informs the complainant, but may also continue with an investigation.

Delegation of decision-making

The Ombudsman has 2 deputies and 6 directors below them. They may undertake any function authorised by the Ombudsman including rejecting complaints at the screening stage or issuing reports.

Following up complaints

Where a remedy has been agreed in principle but without setting figures, the outcome is followed up with the government department for the purposes of the *Annual Report*.

Complaining about the scheme itself

Complainants not satisfied with the way the Ombudsman has dealt with the complaint (though not including the decision of the Ombudsman) can contact the select committee for the Parliamentary Commissioner.

3. The scheme's structure and administration

Origins and membership

A statutory scheme, established under the Parliamentary Commissioner Act 1967 as amended by the Parliamentary and Health Service Commissioners Act 1987 and the Parliamentary Commissioner Act 1994. Started operating in April 1967.

Structure and accountability

The Ombudsman is accountable to parliament through the select committee on the Parliamentary Commissioner for Administration.

The Select Committee

Membership

MPs.

Role

To take evidence from the Ombudsman and bodies within the Ombudsman's jurisdiction; to take evidence on the Ombudsman's annual and other reports; to carry out more general or thematic enquiries, for example into the operation of the code of practice on access to government information. Meets regularly.

The Ombudsman

Appointment

By the Queen, following open competition, on the recommendation of the government agreed with the leader of the Opposition and the chairman of the House of Commons select committee on the Parliamentary Commissioner for Administration. May be removed by the Queen, if asked to do so by parliament.

Term of appointment

Up to age 65.

Role

Responsibility for running the office and complaints-handling. The Parliamentary Ombudsman also holds the post of Health Service Ombudsman and the two schemes have a joint office.

Scheme's terms of reference

Set out in legislation (the Parliamentary Commissioner Act 1967 as amended); change would require amending legislation.

Monitoring

Standards of service are published in the *Annual Report*.

Research has been undertaken into the extent of public awareness of the scheme and the satisfaction of complainants. Summaries are available from the Ombudsman's office.

BIOA member?

Yes.

Funding

Funded by parliament. The budget is negotiated directly with the Treasury.

Costs

Running cost

£15 million including health service costs.

Cost per complaint

For 1995, the forecast was £218 per enquiry, £15,229 per case. No current figures available.

Staffing

Overall responsibility

The Ombudsman.

Staff

2 deputy Ombudsmen, 99 investigative staff and 440 admin staff, including those of the Health Service Commissioner. Staff hold a mixture of permanent posts, secondments from the organisations within jurisdiction, and fixed term contracts.

Forthcoming changes

The 1996 report by Lord Woolf, *Access to Justice*, recommended a change in the law to allow the Ombudsman to refer cases to the courts and vice versa.

Improving best practice

The Ombudsman can report on issues raised by many complainants on the same area of administration. His views are sought on a range of issues of parliamentary interest. He has considerable effect in causing procedures to be changed to improve standards of service and the handling of complaints at local level. An advisory booklet is published for the staff of organisations covered.

Facts and figures

New complaints received in writing (including ineligible complaints)

Subject of complaint	1995[1]	1996
Department of Social Security	834	908
Inland Revenue	160	237
Department of the Environment	67	54
Department of Transport	64	63
Legal Aid Board	63	74
Department for Education and Employment	54	58
Lord Chancellor's Department	44	64
Customs and Excise	40	28
Home Office	34	36
Department of Trade and Industry	29	48
Scottish Office	22	20
Ministry of Agriculture, Fisheries and Food	22	21
Ministry of Defence	20	14
Other	87	60

[1] Includes 44 complaints concerning access to official information.

Numbers of complaints at each stage of procedure

	1995	1996
New complaints received	1,706	1,920
Cases not pursued past initial screening	1,226	1,413
Investigations discontinued	3	6
Full investigations concluded	245	260

Outcome of complaints fully investigated

Complaints justified	153 (62%)	189 (58%)
Complaints partly justified	83 (34%)	57 (31%)
Complaints not justified	9 (4%)	14 (11%)

Information available about the scheme

Publicising the scheme

Books, posters and a leaflet in a wide range of languages are widely available to advice bureaux, public bodies and solicitors' offices.

Press releases accompany the publication of all reports; press coverage has increased markedly in recent years. The broadcasting and televising of the proceedings of the select committee raise public awareness of the scheme. Senior members of staff are regularly invited to speak at meetings and conferences.

Terms of reference

Set out in the Parliamentary Commissioner Act 1967, as amended.

Annual Report

Usually published in March. In addition to the tables above it includes: historical information on workloads; an analysis of outcome of investigations by organisation concerned; a list of injustices remedied by organisation; output and performance targets; further information on cases not fully investigated; forecasts of costs per enquiry and per case; and a bibliography.

Other publications

HMSO, *The Ombudsman in Your Files*, Office of Public Service, 1995.

Select Committee on the Parliamentary Commissioner for Administration, *Maladministration and Redress*, First Report, 1994-95, HC 112, January 1995.

Select Committee on the Parliamentary Commissioner for Administration, *The Powers, Work and Jurisdiction of the Ombudsman*, First Report 1993-94, HC 33, November 1993.

Select Committee on the Parliamentary Commissioner for Administration, *The Implications of the Citizen's Charter for the Work of the Parliamentary Commissioner for Administration*, Second Report 1991-92, HC 158, February 1992.

de Smith, Jowell and Woolf, 'Judicial Review of Administrative Action', in Birkinshaw, *Grievances, Remedies and the State*, Sweet and Maxwell, 1985.

HMSO also publishes volumes of selected investigation cases (the parties are not identified) and occasionally special reports on cases of particular public interest with important implications for public services, for example the Child Support Agency.

Northern Ireland Ombudsman

(The Parliamentary Ombudsman for Northern Ireland and the Northern Ireland Commissioner for Complaints)

33 Wellington Place, Belfast BT1 6HN
Freepost: The Ombudsman, Freepost, Belfast BT1 6BR
Tel: 01232 233 821. Freephone: 0800 343424
Fax: 01232 234912
E-mail: ombudsman@nics.gov.uk
Web site: http://ombudsman.nics.gov.uk

Ombudsman: Gerry Burns MBE

1. Using the scheme: key points

The Northern Ireland Ombudsman is both the Parliamentary Ombudsman and the Commissioner for Complaints. This entry covers both complaints schemes.

Service-providers covered

The Parliamentary Ombudsman

All Northern Ireland government departments including departmental agencies (such as Social Security, the Child Support Agency and Driver and Vehicle Testing).

The Commissioner for Complaints

The Housing Executive, local councils and many other local and public bodies (all listed in the scheme's information leaflet).

Health and social services boards, health service trusts and other health-related bodies. The Equal Opportunities Commission for Northern Ireland and the Fair Employment Commission for Northern Ireland.

Complaints covered

Complaints that administrative failures (or 'maladministration') have resulted in a personal injustice to the complainant.

Complaints not covered

'Frivolous and vexatious' complaints.

Complaints concerning fair employment (religious or political) and equal opportunities (sex discrimination) which do not involve administrative failure.

Complaints about doctors, dentists and other health professionals in connection with health care, such as the type of treatment received (but see Forthcoming changes below).

Complaints made about the security forces.

Cases on which a court has already ruled, those already subject to court proceedings or those in which court action is contemplated.

Who can complain?

Private individuals, groups of individuals, businesses, partnerships, charities and unincorporated bodies.

A representative can complain on behalf of someone else, provided there is good reason why the person is unable to pursue the complaint.

A representative can complain on behalf of a dead person.

One public body cannot complain about another. Individual members cannot complain about a public body of which they are or were a member at the time the complaint arose.

Cost

Free to complainants.

Geographical limits

The complainant must either currently be a resident of Northern Ireland (or, if dead, a resident at the time of death), or must have been a resident or present in Northern Ireland at the time of the events from which the complaint arises.

Time limits

Complaints must be lodged not later than 12 months from the day on which the complainant was first aware of the problem.

The Ombudsman can investigate complaints outside this time limit if there are special circumstances (for instance, if the complainant has been actively pursuing the matter without success).

Remedies

Financial compensation

Can include awards for financial loss, compensation for loss of interest, and consolation for worry, distress or inconvenience. No maximum amount. (The average award in 1996: £468. Largest actual award in the scheme's lifetime: £13,233.)

If the Ombudsman holds a formal hearing, the complainant may be paid any necessary expenses (paid once in the last 2 years).

May reduce the amount of compensation if the actions of the complainant contributed to the problem. (This fact would also be taken into consideration in reaching the actual decision.)

Other

The Ombudsman can recommend corrective action or an apology.

2. The complaints procedure

Making the complaint

Complaints to the Parliamentary Ombudsman scheme must be referred by an MP.

Complainants have direct access to the Commissioner for Complaints scheme. They do not need to use an intermediary.

Complaints must be in writing, although oral complaints are acceptable to start the process off.

There is no standard complaint form, but a guidance leaflet is available. Staff will give all necessary help to those who have difficulty making a complaint.

Exhausting the internal complaints procedure

Complainants must first exhaust all internal channels of complaint. The Ombudsman usually asks the organisation concerned to confirm that this has been done. However, the Ombudsman has the power to waive this requirement if he thinks it would be unreasonable in the circumstances. If a complainant is dissatisfied with the internal complaints system, the Ombudsman's staff may be able to offer advice and information about approaching the Ombudsman.

Powers of investigation

Powers to call and examine witnesses, and to require the production of documents.

Criteria for decisions

Considers the position in law, and whether or not the provider's action was proper or improper. (In practice, the Ombudsman places most emphasis on the seriousness of the maladministration and on the level of injustice suffered.)

The Ombudsman is not bound by previous decisions, but is aware of those where the circumstances and constraints were similar.

Confidentiality

The Ombudsman does not copy either party's correspondence to the other but does, where appropriate, quote detailed extracts in his investigation report.

The names of all bodies against whom complaints are received are published in the *Annual Report*. Noteworthy cases are also summarised. However, no details are released which could identify the complainant.

Stages in complaint resolution

Preliminary enquiries

Can be made at any time. For complaints not within the scheme's remit, staff will offer information and advice on how to proceed: they may refer the complainant to any other appropriate system or body, in the public or private sector, and sometimes forward a complaint automatically.

Enquiry stage

On receiving an eligible complaint, screening officers examine any supporting documentary evidence and make enquiries to determine whether there appears to be evidence of an injustice arising from maladministration. Their decisions are usually based on written evidence, although they sometimes also interview officials.

If there is no evidence of maladministration causing injustice, the complainant will usually receive a rejection letter. But if that letter would run to more than two A4-size pages, or if there is evidence of maladministration but no recurring substantive injustice or system flaw, a more formal 'enquiry report' will be issued to both parties.

Formal investigation

If the screening officers detect what appears to be evidence of maladministration and a substantive injustice or system flaw, the complaint will be formally investigated.

Report stage

A draft report is issued at the end of the formal investigation. The draft goes to the permanent secretary and the chief executive of the body complained about, so that they can comment on the factual accuracy and reasonableness of the proposed findings. They must usually respond within 3 weeks.

Where he is acting as Commissioner for Complaints (which excludes government departments and agencies), the Ombudsman must inform the public body about any adverse comments he proposes to make about it. The body then has the right to ask for a formal hearing. If there is a hearing, the complainant also gets a copy of the draft report and the opportunity to ask for a similar hearing. (Hearings take place in the Ombudsman's office.) A formal enquiry report is then issued to both parties.

Special report

Issued only if a government department or agency fails to comply with a recommendation made in a formal report. (The Ombudsman has never had to issue a special report.)

Progress reports

Cases are reviewed with complainants at various stages during a formal investigation.

Types of ruling

Informal settlement

More than 90% of complaints received by the scheme are dealt with informally: of these, a small number are settled and around 60% are rejected as showing no evidence of maladministration.

Recommendation

Of the cases that do proceed to formal investigation (3% in 1996), the Ombudsman makes a recommendation in most of them (90% in 1996; the remaining 10% were not upheld). Recommendations are not binding on the body against which the complaint has been brought.

Rights of appeal against a decision

There is no right of appeal within the scheme.

The scheme is subject to judicial review (although there have been none).

The Parliamentary Ombudsman

There is no further action the complainant can take if he or she remains dissatisfied, apart from writing to the parliamentary select committee to which the Ombudsman reports (see Structure and accountability below) or applying for a judicial review.

The Commissioner for Complaints

A complainant who remains dissatisfied (either with the remedy recommended by the Ombudsman or with a public body's failure to implement a recommendation) can apply to the county court. The court cannot re-hear the case, but it can vary the amount of compensation awarded or order compliance with a recommendation. (See Failure to comply with rulings below.)

Failure to comply with rulings

The Parliamentary Ombudsman

The presence of the parliamentary select committee is an incentive for government departments and agencies to comply with the Ombudsman's rulings. (In practice there have been no failures to comply.)

The Commissioner for Complaints

The complainant can apply to the county court. In practice, the county court has been asked to increase the amount of a compensation award but not to enforce a ruling. (See Rights of appeal above.)

How long does the process take?

Target timescale

Screening a complaint - 3 weeks; formal investigation - 32 weeks.

Actual timescale

Screening a complaint - 3 weeks; formal investigation - 34.2 weeks.

There is a fast-track procedure for complaints where the maladministration is not significant or the injustice is not serious and where the public body can take immediate corrective action. In these cases, there is no formal investigation, but enquiries are made (resulting in an enquiry report or a settlement letter).

Delegation of decision-making

When he is absent, the Ombudsman delegates his powers to the Deputy Ombudsman. Otherwise the Ombudsman approves all decision letters and reports, except those telling complainants that their cases are outside the scheme's jurisdiction: these are signed by designated officers.

Following up complaints

If there is a likelihood of non-compliance, the Ombudsman checks that his recommendations have been implemented.

Complaining about the scheme itself

The Ombudsman replies to complaints with an explanatory letter. No record is kept of the numbers of complaints and whether or not they were upheld.

Complainants about the Parliamentary Ombudsman can contact the select committee (see Structure and accountability below).

3. The scheme's structure and administration

Origins and membership

Started operating in 1969. Both are statutory schemes. The most recent establishing legislation is the Ombudsman (Northern Ireland) Order 1996 and the Commissioner for Complaints (Northern Ireland) Order 1996.

Structure and accountability

The Northern Ireland Ombudsman is responsible for two complaints-handling schemes, each accountable in different ways.

As Parliamentary Ombudsman, the Ombudsman's *Annual Report* is subject to the scrutiny of the Parliamentary Select Committee for the Commissioner of Administration.

Membership

MPs.

Role

To protect the Ombudsman's independence; particularly helpful in ensuring that the Ombudsman's recommendations are accepted and implemented by government departments. Plays no part in policy, strategy or implementation (for which the Ombudsman alone is responsible).

As Commissioner for Complaints, the Ombudsman is accountable to parliament and must, by law, issue it with an *Annual Report* (but is not questioned on it by a select committee or any other body).

Expenditure for both schemes is monitored by the Department of Finance and Personnel of the Northern Ireland Office.

The Ombudsman

Appointment

By the Queen on the government's recommendation. Can be removed either because he is incapable of performing the duties of the office or by asking to be relieved of those duties.

Term of appointment

Up to age 65.

Role

Overall responsibility for running the office and complaints-handling.

Scheme's terms of reference

Laid down by statute. Can only be changed by amending legislation.

Monitoring

Standards of service are published in the *Annual Report*. A public awareness campaign was completed in 1995. A client satisfaction survey was carried out in 1996.

BIOA member?

Yes.

Funding

The Ombudsman's salary is funded by parliament through the consolidated fund. The scheme's operational costs are included in the Northern Ireland block grant.

Costs

Running cost

£505,000 in 1996 (£440,000 in 1995).

Cost per complaint

Not routinely published.

Staffing

Overall responsibility

The Ombudsman.

Staff

There is a Deputy Ombudsman, appointed by the Ombudsman. Usually a secondment from the public service, for a fixed term of 3 years. 7 investigation officers divided into two teams, each headed by a director: one team deals with screening, the other with investigations. 5 support staff, all reporting to a deputy principal. (All staff are seconded from the civil service.)

Forthcoming changes

The scheme's jurisdiction was extended in 1996 to cover more departmental agencies and public bodies. There is likely to be amending legislation to provide for health complaints about clinical misjudgment and to include family health service practitioners.

Improving best practice

Government departments and agencies are advised about flaws in their systems and procedures. The Ombudsman's enquiry reports promote best practice.

Facts and figures

New complaints received in writing (including ineligible complaints)

Subject of complaint[1]	1995	1996	% change
Personnel	18	29	61
Water/Drainage/Sewerage	7	6	-14
Planning	41	52	27
Social security benefits	71	61	-14
Education/Libraries	50	39	-22
Local government	59	63	7
Health/Social Services	79	72	-9
Housing	134	150	12
Miscellaneous	135	165	22

[1] All categories may also include some complaints concerning personnel matters.

Numbers of complaints at each stage of procedure

	1995	1996	% change
Total complaints handled[1]	595	637	7
Complaints not pursued (eg. because not within remit or referred elsewhere)	546	596	9
Formal investigations	53	43	-19

Outcome of formal investigations

Complaints upheld	40 (82%)	24 (77%)	-
Complaint upheld in part	3 (6%)	4 (13%)	-
Complaint not upheld	6 (12%)	3 (10%)	-

[1] Figures do not tie up because not all cases submitted for formal investigation were reported in the same year.

Information available about the scheme

Publicising the scheme

There is no statutory obligation to inform complainants of the existence of the scheme, but the Ombudsman gives high priority to an information awareness campaign, with advertisements in all media.

The scheme publishes a publicity leaflet and occasional press releases on newsworthy cases. The Ombudsman gives lectures and attends 'information clinics' around Northern Ireland.

Terms of reference

Published in the relevant legislation (see Structure and accountability above).

Annual Report

Usually published February or March. In addition to the tables above, it includes information on historical trends, analyses of complaints by public body complained of, further information on time taken to deal with complaints, and analyses of cases not formally investigated.

Office of the Ombudsman, Republic of Ireland

52 St Stephen's Green, Dublin 2
Tel: 003531 678 5222. Fax: 00 3531 661 0570
Web site: http://www.irlgov.ie/ombudsman
E-mail: ombudsman@ombudsman.irhgov.ie

Ombudsman: Kevin Murphy

1. Using the scheme: key points

Service-providers covered

The civil service, local authorities, health boards, postal and telecommunications services in the Irish Republic.

Complaints covered

Complaints about any administrative action which has adversely affected the complainant (or may do so). The action must fall within the definition of 'maladministration' in the Ombudsman Act 1980: it might be a decision, a refusal or failure to take action, or an administrative procedure.

Complaints not covered

Complaints about commercial decisions (although the way the decision was taken might be covered).

Cases concerning actions taken in connection with clinical judgment by doctors.

The 'reserved functions of local authorities' - for example, the functions exercised by elected representatives, such as setting rates.

Complaints relating to recruitment, pay and conditions of employment.

Complaints about the actions of the police force or in the running of prisons, or issues of national security or military activity.

Cases where there is a right of appeal to an independent tribunal or appeal body (such as the Appeal Commissioners of Income Tax). However, the Ombudsman may investigate the complaints if he believes that special circumstances make it proper to do so.

Complaints concerning court decisions or matters which are already the subject of court proceedings. However, the Ombudsman may investigate the complaint if he believes that special circumstances make it proper to do so.

Who can complain?

Private individuals, groups of people, businesses, partnerships, charities and other unincorporated bodies.

Friends, relatives and legal representatives on behalf of an individual, with that individual's consent.

Personal representatives, beneficiaries and relatives on behalf of a dead person.

Cost

Free to complainants.

Geographical limits

Complaints must be against the bodies in the Republic of Ireland listed above (see Service-providers covered). There is no restriction on the complainant's place of residence.

Time limits

Complaints must reach the Ombudsman within 12 months of the action which caused the problem or, if later, within 12 months of the complainant becoming aware of the action.

The Ombudsman can decide to accept complaints after 12 months if he believes that special circumstances make it proper to do so.

Remedies

Financial compensation

Compensation for financial loss, distress and inconvenience. There is no maximum amount. (Typical amounts are less than £2,000, but there was one award of over £8,000 in 1995.)

Compensation can include interest on the amount due and the costs of legal or other expert advice.

The Ombudsman can reduce the amount if he believes that the complainant contributed to the problem.

Other

The Ombudsman can recommend apologies or explanations, and corrective action such as acceptance of a rejected application.

2. The complaints procedure

Making the complaint

Complainants can approach the scheme direct or through an intermediary such as an elected representative. Complaints can be in writing, in person, by telephone or by e-mail. There is no standard complaint form, although there is a guidance leaflet. If someone has difficulty making a complaint, they will be given appropriate help - for example, a home visit or a complaint taken down from dictation.

The office has a policy of dealing with complainants in his or her own language (in practice, the only other language used is Irish).

Exhausting the internal complaints procedure

Before using the scheme, complainants must have exhausted all internal channels of complaint, although there is no set procedure for deciding when this stage has been reached. This requirement can be waived in urgent cases (for example, a basic needs payment complaint made approaching a weekend).

Powers of investigation

The Ombudsman can compel the production of any information or evidence relevant to the investigation, and can compel any person to attend an interview. The underlying legislation prohibits anybody from obstructing the Ombudsman, or from doing anything which would count as contempt of court if the case were before a court.

Criteria for decisions

In practice, most emphasis is placed on the principles of good administration and the rights of citizens (which are set out in the *Annual Reports*). Decisions are not limited to strictly legal criteria.

Each case is decided on its merits. The Ombudsman seeks to be consistent in decision-making, but is not bound by previous decisions.

Confidentiality

During an investigation, material provided by one side is not routinely copied to the other, unless the other party's comments are sought. The complainant can submit material in confidence, although this may not bear as much weight as evidence that can be disclosed.

Noteworthy cases are published in the *Annual Report* - complainants are not identified by name, the bodies concerned are.

Stages in complaint resolution

Screening

New complaints are screened by the support unit, to establish whether they are within jurisdiction. Further information may be needed from complainants and it may be necessary to interview them.

Cases not within the scheme's remit are automatically forwarded to any other appropriate body.

Preliminary examination

Assuming that the case appears to be within remit, the body against which the complaint is brought is asked for a report (within 2 weeks). Once the report is received, further correspondence, a copy of the body's file, telephone contact, interviews of those concerned or a site inspection may be used to resolve outstanding queries. The complainant and the body may accept a satisfactory settlement at this stage.

Report

Once the information-gathering process is over, the investigator considers the case and (except for routine cases) draws up a report. The report recommends whether (a) the case should be closed, (b) the body concerned should be given a final opportunity to deal with the matter, (c) legal advice should be sought or (d) a formal investigation should be carried out. Complex cases may need to be discussed with a senior investigator or the Ombudsman. If formal investigation is recommended, the Ombudsman approves the decision.

If the case is closed at this stage a final letter (which, depending on the complexity of the case, may be signed by the Ombudsman, the investigator or the support unit) is sent to the complainant. The complainant can bring forward new evidence or arguments and ask the Ombudsman to look at the case again if unhappy with the decision.

Formal investigation

This takes place where (a) the body involved has been given every opportunity to put things right voluntarily and there appears to be evidence of its failing/wrongdoing or (b) where it is the only satisfactory method of establishing the facts of the case. An investigation may also be necessary where the complainant has received redress but there is still a question of maladministration.

The investigator prepares an investigation plan. The body concerned is sent a statement setting out the basis of the complaint and must respond within 14 days (although it is usually possible to extend this period). Interviews are then held with the relevant officials and sometimes the complainant. (Hearings of both parties at the same time are not held.) When all issues are clarified as far as possible, the investigator will prepare a draft of the Ombudsman's report.

Draft report

Extracts from the draft report which are critical of officials are sent to them for their comments. The draft report (including factual summary and findings but excluding any recommendations) is sent to the body concerned, for factual comments and any final observations and to give them a chance to undertake a final review. The draft report is not sent to the complainant (although parts of the report would be sent to the complainant if a detailed statement by the complainant were crucial to the final outcome). Two weeks is usually allowed for responses.

Final report

This includes any recommendations and is signed by the Ombudsman. The body concerned has 14 days in which to tell the Ombudsman how it intends to implement his recommendations. If it fails to do this to the Ombudsman's satisfaction, he has the power to lay a special report before parliament (this has never proved necessary).

Progress reports

Progress reports are sent to the complainant at the end of each stage in the procedure.

Types of ruling

Informal conciliation

Over 90% of complaints are resolved in this way at the preliminary examination stage.

Formal investigation followed by non-binding recommendation

The remaining 10% of cases are settled in this way.

Rights of appeal against a decision

There is no right to require the Ombudsman to reconsider his final decision. There is, however, an internal appeal mechanism for reviewing cases where a complainant is unhappy with the decision. There is no right of appeal to an external body.

Complainants retain their right to take legal action if not satisfied.

The scheme is subject to judicial review but there have been none in its lifetime.

The Ombudsman cannot at present refer particular questions to the courts to resolve an important legal point (but this is under review).

Failure to comply with rulings

Where the Ombudsman believes the response to a recommendation is not satisfactory he can make a special report to both houses of parliament (this has never been necessary).

How long does the process take?

Target timescale

90 to 180 days from receipt to completion of examination.

Actual timescale

139 days.

The process can be accelerated for urgent welfare cases concerning basic needs payments and emergency housing needs.

Delegation of decision-making

The scheme's director represents the Ombudsman in his absence. All the Ombudsman's complaints-handling functions are delegated to the director and to investigators. The Ombudsman does not sign, or read through, every decision letter.

Following up complaints

Complaints that are not within the scheme's remit are not followed up.

When the Ombudsman makes a recommendation, a response is required from the body concerned stating how it proposes to implement the recommendation. The office checks that recommendations are implemented.

Complaining about the scheme itself

Every aspect of any complaint, and the manner in which the case was handled, is reviewed personally by the Ombudsman. (Complaints about the scheme's service are very rare: none has so far been upheld.)

3. The scheme's structure and administration

Origins and membership

A statutory scheme set up under the Ombudsman Act 1980. Started operating in July 1984.

Structure and accountability

There is no body which oversees the scheme.

The Ombudsman

Appointment

Appointed by the President of Ireland on the nomination of both houses of parliament. Can be dismissed by the President for misbehaviour, incapacity or bankruptcy, following resolutions passed by both houses of parliament calling for his removal.

Term of appointment

Initially 6 years, with reappointment allowed for a second or subsequent term. Must be under the age of 61 on appointment, and must retire at 67.

Role

> Responsible for running the office (but this is delegated to the scheme's director) and for complaints-handling.

Scheme's terms of reference

> These are set out in the Ombudsman Act 1980. Can only be changed by amending legislation, except that the bodies covered by the scheme can be changed by affirmative order passed by both houses of parliament.

Monitoring

> The scheme monitors complainant satisfaction through questionnaires but its findings are not published in detail.

BIOA member?

> Yes.

Funding

> The Minister for Finance proposes an annual budget which is voted by parliament.

Costs

Running cost

> £1.104 million in 1995 (estimate for 1996: £1.391 million).

Cost per complaint

> Not published.

Staffing

Overall responsibility

> The director, who is a civil servant of the state (as distinct from the government) has responsibility for running the office. He is the financial accounting officer and is statutorily accountable to parliament in this capacity. All the Ombudsman's functions are delegated to the director, except for

the making of the Ombudsman's *Annual Report* or a special report to the houses of parliament.

Staff

16 investigative staff with qualifications in a range of areas, including law, accountancy, public administration, language and psychology. 22 administration and support staff.

Forthcoming changes

At the time of going to press, the Irish government was considering an amendment to the Ombudsman Act to extend the Ombudsman's remit and increase his powers. Matters under consideration include:

- extending the scheme's jurisdiction to include all bodies which receive more than 50% of their funding from the Exchequer;

- the power to make general recommendations about public administration;

- the power to take evidence on oath;

- the power to initiate civil proceedings;

- the power to state a case to the High Court for an opinion.

Improving best practice

No specific legal powers to improve best practice. However, in recent years the scheme has assumed the role of improving standards of public administration. For example, in his 1996 *Annual Report*, the Ombudsman published a Guide to Standards of Best Practice for Public Servants. The Guide explains how to deal promptly, fairly and impartially with the public. The scheme is represented on committees advising on complaints procedures in the legal, health and education fields, and on committees which advise the government on issues such as open and transparent service delivery and quality customer service. It is extremely unlikely that the views and opinions of the Ombudsman on good administrative practice would be ignored.

Facts and figures

Numbers of complaints completed[1]

Subject of complaint	1994	1995	% change
Unemployment assistance	129	91	-29
Old age pension	97	77	-21
Other social welfare	451	382	-15
Income tax	86	72	-16
Other revenue commissioners	59	47	-20
Headage and other livestock grants	79	154	95
Other agriculture, food and forestry	40	49	23
Higher education grants	31	23	-26
Other education	48	38	-21
Environment	24	33	38
Housing allocation and transfers	61	80	31
Planning enforcement	53	64	21
Other local authorities	339	408	20
Supplementary welfare allowance	141	88	-38
Disabled person's maintenance allowance	65	39	-40
Other health boards	156	125	-20
Telephone accounts	199	188	-6
Other telecom	87	72	-17
Postal delivery	31	35	13
Other postal	48	27	-44

[1] Full information on complaints received not available. Complaint types are categorised on the basis of complaints completed.

Numbers of complaints at each stage of procedure

	1994	1995	% change
Total new complaints	3,160	2,879	-9.00
Total complaints handled	3,130	3,059	-2.25
Complaints not within remit/referred elsewhere	671	629	-6.25
Complaints withdrawn/discontinued	413	394	-4.60
Complaints completed (whether by settlement or formal recommendation)	1,908	1,787	-6.35

Outcome of complaints fully investigated [1]

Complaint upheld	414 (22%)	403 (23%)	-
Complaint upheld in part	580 (30%)	542 (30%)	-
Complaint not upheld	914 (48%)	842 (47%)	-

[1] Includes examinations and investigations.

Information available about the scheme

Publicising the scheme

One of the 'citizens' rights' set out by the Ombudsman is the right to be told what remedies are open to them.

Guidance leaflet and school posters are widely available.

The scheme organises publicity campaigns and regional visits backed up by radio and press advertising. The Ombudsman is considering publishing regular bulletins.

Terms of reference

Published in the Ombudsman Act 1980, in information leaflets and on the Ombudsman's web site.

Annual Report

Published in May or June. As well as the tables above, includes analyses of complaints received which are outside jurisdiction, further information on the subjects of complaints, breakdowns for each body covered, and further information on caseflows.

Other publications

The following publications are written by, and available from, the Ombudsman.

Quality in Health Care - the Patient's Perspective, November 1996.

The Role of a National Ombudsman in the Supervision of the Application of European Community Law, September 1996.

Quality in Local Government, June 1996.

The Evolving Role of the Irish Ombudsman, March 1996.

Information and the Public Service, February 1996.

Possibilities to Improve the Impact of the Work of Ombudsmen and Ombudswomen, June 1995.

Good and Fair Administration - A View from the Ombudsman's Office, January 1995.

Health Service Ombudsman

(The Health Service Commissioner for England, Scotland and Wales)

For England: Millbank Tower, Millbank, London SW1P 4QP
Tel: 0171 217 4053. Text telephone: 0171 217 4067. Fax: 0171 217 4066

For Scotland: 1st Floor, 28 Thistle Street, Edinburgh EH2 1EN
Tel: 0131 225 7465. Fax: 0131 226 4447

For Wales: Fourth Floor, Pearl Assurance House, Greyfriars Road,
Cardiff CF1 3AG
Tel: 01222 394621. Fax: 01222 226909

Ombudsman: Michael Buckley

There are three Health Service Ombudsman posts. All three, together with the post of Parliamentary Ombudsman, are held by the same person.

1. Using the scheme: key points

Service-providers covered

All national health service authorities, trusts and individuals providing NHS services, including:

- NHS hospitals;

- community health services;

- for events after 31 March 1996, family GPs (including fundholding GPs), dentists, pharmacists and opticians providing NHS services;

- private healthcare providers supplying services by arrangement with NHS bodies.

Complaints covered

Complaints about poor service due to maladministration or administrative failure.

Complaints about the failure to purchase or provide a service to which the complainant is entitled due to maladministration.

Complaints under the codes of practice on openness in the NHS (introduced in June 1995).

For events that occurred after 31 March 1996, complaints concerning clinical judgement (the Ombudsman's booklet *A Guide to the Work of the Health Service Ombudsman* explains how the Ombudsman deals with this topic). For these kinds of complaints, it is not necessary to show maladministration.

After 31 March 1996, in some circumstances, complaints from NHS staff if they feel that they have been treated unreasonably by the NHS during the investigation of a complaint.

Complaints not covered

Complaints about clinical judgement arising from events which took place before 1 April 1996.

Complaints about government departments, such as the Department of Health or the NHS Executive, or about local authority departments, such as social services. (These may be within the jurisdiction of other Ombudsmen - see sections on government and local government.)

Complaints about services in a non-NHS hospital or nursing home, unless the services are paid for by the NHS.

Complaints concerning properly made decisions which the organisation involved has a right to make, even if the complainant does not agree with the decision.

Complaints concerning contractual or commercial matters, unless they relate to services for patients provided under an NHS contract.

Complaints concerning personnel matters, including complaints from NHS staff about their employment.

Usually, complaints for which there are other ways of obtaining a remedy - for example, a right of appeal to an independent tribunal or a right to take a case to the courts (in this context, the professional regulatory bodies, such as the General Medical Council, do not count as tribunals). However, the Ombudsman can decide to investigate if the complainant has not used those other rights, or if he considers that it would be unreasonable to expect them to do so.

Who can complain?

Individuals, groups of individuals, corporate bodies, partnerships, charities, etc. who consider they have suffered hardship or injustice.

A relative or anyone else (including someone who works for the NHS) on behalf of the complainant, provided the person concerned supports the complaint.

A relative, or any other individual or body the Ombudsman regards as suitable, on behalf of a dead person.

Cost

Free to complainants.

Geographical limits

The complaint must be about actions taken by or on behalf of the NHS while the complainant was in the UK. The complainant does not have to be a resident of the UK.

Time limits

Usually, the Ombudsman cannot investigate complaints about events which took place more than 12 months before the complainant first became aware that there might be a cause for complaint. The Ombudsman can decide to waive this time limit in cases where he thinks it reasonable to do so.

Remedies

Financial compensation

The Ombudsman can only recommend financial compensation. He has done this in the few cases (8 in 1995/96) where there has been an identifiable loss or cost as a direct result of maladministration. He can also recommend repayment of unnecessary costs incurred by patients or their families. There are no legal limits on amounts. He does not assess or recommend damages as courts may do as a result of litigation involving medical negligence.

Other

Getting a decision changed, a review of procedures or an apology.

Reporting to a regulator.

Where the Ombudsman considers it necessary to protect the health and safety of patients, he can disclose information discovered about anyone in the course of an investigation to a professional regulatory body (like the General Medical Council) or to the employing health service body.

2. The complaints procedure

Making the complaint

Complainants can approach the Ombudsman direct: they do not need to use an intermediary. Complaints must be in writing. There is no need to use a specific complaint form (although there is one in the scheme leaflet). The Ombudsman's office will help if the complainant has difficulty.

Exhausting the internal complaints procedure

Before bringing a complaint to the Ombudsman, complainants must first pursue it through the organisation's own complaints procedure, and then if still dissatisfied, ask the local NHS trust or health authority for a review of the complaint by an independent panel.

The Ombudsman can decide to investigate complaints that have not completed this two-stage procedure if it has taken too long to deal with the complaint locally or if a panel review was unreasonably refused; he can also consider complaints that a decision to refuse a panel was taken maladministratively and may recommend that it be reconsidered.

Powers of investigation

Has the power to compel witnesses to attend and answer questions, and to call for the production of documents. Organisations covered by the scheme cannot withhold papers on the grounds of a statutory duty of confidentiality, public interest immunity or legal privilege.

Criteria for decisions

The Ombudsman applies the standard of proof that applies to civil cases in court - that is, he reaches decisions on the balance of probabilities.

Confidentiality

Investigations are confidential. No papers are passed to the other party.

Names of complainants are not published in any case reports published by the Ombudsman.

Stages in complaint resolution

Screening

New complaints are screened to establish whether they are within jurisdiction. This may reveal the need for additional information, and occasionally the screening staff may contact the organisation informally to check out the background to a complaint.

Where cases are not within the Ombudsman's remit complainants are advised of any appropriate alternative body they could approach.

Statement of complaint

Where he investigates, the Ombudsman must give the NHS body or practitioner complained against an opportunity to comment. A statement of complaint is drawn up by the Ombudsman's office and sent for comment, with a copy to the complainant. Organisations are expected to give their initial comments within 3 weeks.

Investigation

> After receiving the organisation's initial reply, the investigating officer may conduct interviews with the complainant, relevant NHS staff and anyone else who may be able to assist. All relevant papers will be studied.

Draft report

> Following the investigation, a draft report is produced setting out the evidence and, in most cases, provisional findings and a conclusion. This is sent to the relevant NHS body to check the accuracy of the facts and for comments on their presentation and - if the Ombudsman has upheld the complaint - to seek their agreement to the remedy he proposes.

Final report

> After any changes have been made in the light of comments received, a final report is sent to the NHS body concerned and to the complainant. If the report is not accepted by the NHS body, the Ombudsman may make a special report to parliament, and the NHS body may have to appear before the select committee on the Parliamentary Commissioner for Administration.

Progress reports

> The complainant is sent periodic updates directly.

Types of ruling

Non-binding recommendation

> In cases where the Ombudsman issues a report, he may recommend that the NHS body concerned pursues a particular course of action. The majority of cases received (around 85% in 1996) are not accepted for investigation. This is not necessarily an outright rejection: it may be because the case is settled to the complainant's satisfaction at the screening stage or because the complainant has not exhausted the internal complaints procedures.

Rights of appeal against a decision

There is no appeal against a decision not to investigate a complaint. The Ombudsman can be subject to judicial review

An investigation cannot be re-opened after a report has been issued - but the Ombudsman can decide to open a new investigation if significant new evidence becomes available.

The Ombudsman cannot currently refer cases to the courts (but see Forthcoming changes below).

Failure to comply with rulings

Non-acceptance of the findings and recommendations of the Ombudsman are very rare.

How long does the process take?

Target timescale

Not published at present.

Actual timescale

In 1995/96 screening a complaint took about 5 weeks on average (63% in 18 days). For a full investigation and report - 66 weeks.

Delegation of decision-making

The Ombudsman has 2 deputies and 5 directors and delegates decision-making as he sees fit.

Following up complaints

NHS bodies are asked to confirm that they have acted on any recommendations within three months.

Complaining about the scheme itself

Complaints are made to the Ombudsman.

3. The scheme's structure and administration

Origins and membership

A statutory scheme established under the National Health Service (Scotland) Act 1972 and the National Health Service Reorganisation Act 1973. These were consolidated in the Health Service Commissioners Act 1993 and new powers were added by the Health Service Commissioners (Amendment) Act 1996.

Started operating in October 1973.

Structure and accountability

The Ombudsman is accountable to parliament through the select committee for the Parliamentary Commission for Administration.

Membership

MPs.

Role

To take evidence from the Ombudsman and bodies within the Ombudsman's jurisdiction; to take evidence on the Ombudsman's annual and other reports; to carry out more general or thematic enquiries, for example into the operation of the code of practice on openness in the NHS. Meets regularly.

The Ombudsman

Appointment

By the Crown, on the recommendation of the government agreed with the leader of the Opposition and the chairman of the select committee on the Parliamentary Commissioner for Administration. May be removed by the Queen, if asked to do so by parliament.

Term of appointment

Must retire in 65th year.

Role

Responsibility for running the office and complaints-handling. The Health Service Ombudsman also holds the post of Parliamentary Ombudsman and the two schemes have a joint office.

Scheme's terms of reference

The scheme was set up under an act of parliament and any changes would require amending legislation.

Monitoring

Standards of service are published in the *Annual Report*.

BIOA member?

Yes.

Funding

Funded by parliament. The budget is negotiated directly with the Treasury.

Costs

Running cost

Not given.

Cost per complaint

Not given.

Staffing

Overall responsibility

Not given.

Staff

Appointments are a mixture of permanent posts, secondments from government departments and the NHS, and fixed term contracts. The office has 6 internal professionals, 4 advisers, and appoints external professional assessors on a case-by-case basis.

Forthcoming changes

The 1996 report by Lord Woolf, *Access to Justice*, recommended a change in the law to allow the Ombudsman to refer cases to the courts and vice versa.

Improving best practice

The Ombudsman can report on issues raised by many complainants on the same area of administration. His views are sought on a range of issues of health service interest. He has considerable effect in causing procedures to be changed to improve standards of service and the handling of complaints at local level.

Facts and figures

Numbers of complaints in completed investigations

Subject of complaint	1994/95	1995/96	% change
Admission, discharge and transfer arrangements	28	47	68.0
Equipment and aids	6	8	33.0
Appointments, waiting lists and delay	24	21	-13.0
Attitude	30	26	-13.0
Care and treatment	131	121	-7.6
Communication, consent and counselling	93	83	-11.0
Independent professional review administration	3	14	367.0
Policy decisions and extra contractual referral	2	7	250.0
Patients' property and expenses	8	7	-14.0
Privacy, breach of confidence	3	4	33.0
Records, medical certificates	40	23	-43.0
Hospital complaints handling	131	147	12.2
Other	9	38	322.0

Numbers of complaints at each stage of procedure

	1994/95	1995/96	% change
New complaints received	1,782	1784	0
Cases rejected	429	736	72
Cases outside jurisdiction	182	159	-12
Cases discontinued or withdrawn	38	34	-11
Full investigations concluded	178	229	29

Outcome of complaints fully investigated[1]

Complaints upheld wholly or in part	306 (60%)	338 (62%)	-
Complaints not justified	202 (40%)	208 (38%)	-

[1] These figures reflect the number of case files set up and may differ from the number of investigations concluded because individuals may have more than one complaint.

Information available about the scheme

Publicising the scheme

There is a scheme leaflet in a range of languages available from advice bureaux, public and health service bodies and solicitors' offices, and a *Guide to the Work of the Health Service Ombudsman.*

Terms of reference

In the legislation that set it up.

Annual Report

Usually published in June. In addition to the tables above, includes detailed analysis of: geographical distribution; investigations completed; and cases rejected by reference to powers and jurisdiction, service areas and subject, and professions and subject. Historical information is given on workloads and outcomes.

Other publications

Also publishes, several times a year, volumes of selected investigation cases (the complainants are not identified but the relevant NHS body is).

Independent Housing Ombudsman

3rd Floor, Norman House, 105-109 Strand, London WC2R 0AA
Tel: 0171 836 3630. Lo-call: 0345 125 973
Fax: 0171 836 3900

Ombudsman: Roger Jefferies

This scheme replaced the Housing Association Tenants Ombudsman scheme on 1 April 1997. This entry largely covers the rules of the new scheme, but uses experience and statistics from the old scheme where these could be useful to complainants.

1. Using the scheme: key points

Service-providers covered

All social landlords registered with the Housing Corporation, including housing associations and the newly emerging housing companies, must belong to the scheme.

Other landlords can become members on a voluntary basis.

Complaints covered

All complaints about the duties and services provided by landlords, such as disrepair, harassment, transfers, and how rent and service charges have been decided (but not the actual amount of a rent or service charge rise).

(Under the legislation governing the old scheme, complaints had to concern maladministration - or administrative failures. The Act governing the new scheme does not specifically mention maladministration, but it is likely to be the kind of evidence for which the Ombudsman will be looking.)

Complaints not covered

Commercial decisions.

Complaints about the level or amount of rent and service charge increases (but the Ombudsman can deal with complaints about how they are set).

Disputes between neighbours (but the Ombudsman can deal with complaints about how the landlord dealt with such a dispute).

Complaints against the Housing Corporation.

Frivolous and vexatious cases.

Complaints on which a court has already ruled, or which are already subject to court proceedings, or which are about to go to a court or tribunal. The complainant must choose between using the Ombudsman or court action.

Who can complain?

Private individuals who are tenants or in receipt of services from member landlords.

Relatives, friends or legal representatives can complain on someone else's behalf if that person cannot reasonably do so himself/herself.

Relatives, friends or legal representatives may carry on a complaint on behalf of a dead person - but only if it was already being considered by the Ombudsman before the death and it would be reasonable to complete the investigation.

Groups of people cannot complain, although the Ombudsman can accept 'test cases' such as a residents' association choosing a case whose findings will, they hope, apply to others and, perhaps to all other lessees similarly affected.

Cost

Free to complainants (except, occasionally, for personal expenses when a complaint goes as far as arbitration - see Stages in complaint resolution below).

Geographical limits

Landlords registered with the Housing Corporation in England.

There are separate arrangements for Scotland and Wales, but in practice a small number of English associations still own and manage property in Wales and Scotland and the scheme can deal with complaints concerning these properties.

Tenants who move out of England after the events that gave rise to the complaint can use the scheme.

Time limits

The complaint must have been brought to the attention of the landlord or the Ombudsman within 12 months of the complainant becoming aware of the problem. It must also be brought to the Ombudsman within 12 months of exhausting the landlord's own internal complaints procedure.

Member landlords sometimes allow a complaint to be referred to the Ombudsman outside these time limits.

Remedies

Financial compensation

Can include compensation for financial loss, distress, inconvenience, time and trouble. There is no maximum amount. In practice, under the old scheme, a typical award for distress and inconvenience was £500 (highest actual award in 1995/6 was £4,000). A typical award for financial loss or for time and trouble was around £250 (highest actual award in 1995/6 was £1,000).

The Ombudsman can order the payment of interest on an award, and can also take a complainant's legal or other expert costs into account when assessing the amount of any financial loss.

Takes the complainant's actions into account as a factor in whether or not to award compensation. (For example, a tenant with significant and persistent rent arrears did not receive compensation under the old scheme.)

Other

Can ask for an apology to be made.

Can recommend corrective action such as asking the landlord to reconsider an application for a transfer, or making a recommendation to a member landlord to change its procedures.

2. The complaints procedure

Making the complaint

Complainants can approach the scheme direct: they do not need to use an intermediary.

Complaints can initially be made by phone, which staff will write down and register. Once a complaint is registered, staff usually ask the complainant to fill in a complaint form: a standard form is available, but not compulsory. The Typetalk system can be used for people with hearing and/or speech impairments. Guidance leaflets are available in 10 languages as well as English.

Exhausting the internal complaints procedure

Before the Ombudsman can look into a complaint, the complainant must first exhaust the landlord's internal complaints procedure. The complainant will need a letter from the landlord stating the final position. (Sometimes a landlord will allow the Ombudsman to take on a case without a formal letter.)

Scheme staff can often help tenants before internal channels of complaint have been exhausted. They hold a comprehensive library of landlord's complaints procedures and can send a copy of the relevant procedure to a complainant who has not received one from the landlord. Staff will advise complainants on the internal procedure and what they should do to complete it.

Powers of investigation

For landlords registered with the Housing Corporation the Ombudsman can rely on the Corporation's statutory powers to compel the production of documents and witnesses but in practice this has not been necessary.

For voluntary members of the scheme (that is, landlords who are not registered social landlords) the contract between the member and the scheme gives powers of investigation to the Ombudsman.

Criteria for decisions

From 1 April 1997 the Ombudsman is under a legal duty to decide complaints by reference to what is, in his opinion, fair in all the circumstances of the case. In addition, the scheme is likely to use similar criteria to the old one, namely:

- maladministration, as defined in legal agreements and codes of guidance issued by the Housing Corporation;

- the landlord's own statements of practice;

- the expectations which tenants have of the landlord's performance.

The Ombudsman is not bound by his own previous decisions, but will often take account of them.

Confidentiality

During the investigation of a complaint, letters and supporting evidence from one party will often be copied to the other - but not routinely. Sometimes it will be sufficient for the scheme's investigator to summarise points in a letter. Evidence can be submitted in confidence but this is not encouraged.

The Ombudsman is required to publish his reports of formal inquiries. These reports do not name the complainant but they do name the landlord. They go to the tenant and landlord, any other party which gave evidence, the Housing Corporation and the local housing authority in whose area the landlord's property is based. Where publication of an inquiry report could put even an unnamed complainant at serious risk, the Ombudsman publishes a summary of his findings only. Otherwise, complaints details are confidential.

The Ombudsman publishes an annual digest of cases of interest, including arbitrations and mediations: complainants are not identified.

Stages in complaint resolution

Scrutiny

New complaints are screened by a scrutiny officer who screens out those not within jurisdiction. If the complaint is eligible, the scrutiny officer reports to the casework manager: there is often further correspondence between the scheme, the complainant and the landlord.

For cases outside the scheme's remit, staff refer complainants to the appropriate agency. Any complaints that fall within the regulatory regime of the Housing Corporation are automatically sent on to it.

Enquiries

Each case within jurisdiction is allocated to an investigator, who usually makes enquiries through letters, documents and phone calls, although site visits and interviews are sometimes necessary. The investigator prepares a report for the Ombudsman. The Ombudsman may decide to reject the case, to make a formal inquiry, or - if both parties agree - to arrange for mediation, arbitration (by an external specialist) or informal adjudication (by an in-house investigator). The casework manager might suggest mediation at any point during the scrutiny or enquiry process, if appropriate.

When enquiries lead to a complaint being rejected, a preliminary determination letter is sent to the complainant: the complainant can respond to this, within a 4-week time limit, with any new and significant evidence - otherwise the determination is confirmed.

Formal inquiry

When an investigator recommends a formal inquiry, the Ombudsman may hold a case conference with his staff, then write a brief for the investigation. Inquiries are currently sub-contracted to freelance investigators (although a staff investigator keeps an advisory role). The inquiry may involve examination of files, tape-recorded interviews (sometimes with both landlord and tenant together) and site visits.

Ombudsman's report

Following a formal inquiry, the Ombudsman drafts a report which is sent to both parties and any relevant third party, for comments on its factual accuracy. The final report, including any recommendations, is sent to both parties to the dispute, the Housing Corporation, the local housing authority and anyone else concerned. A formal report may not be issued if the inquiry does not go ahead - for instance, because the case is settled.

Progress reports

Complainants are kept informed of progress at each stage and told when to expect replies. (Under the old scheme, the maximum period without phone or letter contact was 6 weeks.)

Types of ruling

Informal conciliation

20% of complaints were settled in this way under the old scheme in 1995/96.

Mediation

Around 25% of cases in 1995/96 were resolved through mediation, by an external mediator.

Arbitration

Arbitration by an external arbitrator is used in a small number of cases - 6% in 1995/96.

Binding decision

The decision is binding on both parties (15% of cases in 1995/96).

Non-binding recommendation

A non-binding recommendation by the Ombudsman has only recently been introduced (no statistics as yet).

The balance of complaints (33% in 1995/96) are rejected or settled.

Rights of appeal against a decision

There is no right of appeal within the scheme.

A complainant who remains dissatisfied cannot take court action - except following a formal arbitration and then only on restricted grounds.

It is not established whether the scheme is subject to judicial review.

Failure to comply with rulings

In relation to members that are registered landlords, the Ombudsman can rely in part on the enforcement powers of the regulator, the Housing Corporation. (In practice, no landlord has failed to comply with any decisions in the scheme's lifetime.)

Where any member landlord fails to comply, the Ombudsman can require publication of the fact, at the landlord's expense. In addition, any voluntary member that fails to comply can be expelled from the scheme.

The Ombudsman cannot refer a case to the courts to resolve a point of law (although he can refuse to consider a case if he thinks it would be better dealt with by the courts).

How long does the process take?

Target timescale (under the old scheme)

No case to wait for attention for more than 60 days; no formal investigation to wait more than 60 days for commencement; to resolve 75% of cases in 6 months and 90% in 1 year.

Actual timescale (under the old scheme)

Average wait for attention - 30 days; average wait for commencement of formal investigation - 30 days; 60% of cases resolved in 6 months and 90% in 1 year.

Delegation of decision-making

The scheme's casework manager takes all straightforward decisions on whether cases may be referred to mediation (which also needs the consent of the parties concerned). The Ombudsman personally signs, or reads through, all other decision letters.

Following up complaints

The outcome of complaints not within the scheme's jurisdiction are not followed up.

Complaints that reach the scheme before they have exhausted the landlord's internal complaints procedure are followed up, to establish whether the procedure has been completed and that the complainant was satisfied.

In cases resolved by the scheme, the scheme tries to define the compliance required and sets dates by which it expects the landlord to meet the requirements. It follows up with reminders.

Complaining about the scheme itself

The scheme has its own internal complaints procedure. Any complaint is reviewed by the scheme's secretary and lay members of the board. (5 complaints were received in the lifetime of the old scheme, 1 of which was partly upheld. One complaint went to the Parliamentary Ombudsman.)

3. The scheme's structure and administration

Origins and membership

The original scheme - the Housing Association Tenants Ombudsman - started operating in November 1993. It was established by the Housing Corporation, acting under the Housing Association Act 1985. That legislation is now replaced by the Housing Act 1996 which requires registered social landlords to belong to an 'approved Ombudsman scheme'. The new Independent Housing Ombudsman scheme, which started operating on 1 April 1997, is the approved scheme for all social landlords registered with the Housing Corporation. Other landlords can join voluntarily. The new scheme was set up as a company limited by guarantee.

Structure and accountability

The scheme is overseen by the Department of the Environment and the Board of the company.

The Board

Membership

Up to 12 directors - one-third to be representative of landlords, one-third of tenants, and one-third (including the chairman) of the public interest. (The first 4 directors were drawn from the advisory panel for the old scheme; the rest have been appointed by the Board following the code of practice for public appointments.)

Role

To offer advice to the Ombudsman; to monitor the scheme's performance; to comment to the Housing Corporation on resource issues. Plays no part in the resolution of individual complaints. Meets quarterly. Under the old scheme, the advisory panel (equivalent to the new Board) held its meetings in public and in regional venues, a move strongly supported in the public consultation on the terms of the new scheme and which will continue.

The Ombudsman

Appointment

By the Board, subject to the approval of the Secretary of State for the Environment. Can be dismissed by the Secretary of State under the terms of the Housing Act 1996 and by the Board for serious misconduct.

Term of appointment

Initially 4 years, renewable.

Role

Accounting officer and responsibility for complaints-handling.

Scheme's terms of reference

Laid down by the Housing Act 1996. Can be changed if the Board submits amendments for approval by the Secretary of State.

Monitoring

Standards of service are yet to be set for the new scheme.

(Under the old scheme, standards of service were published in the *Annual Report*. Equal opportunities were monitored through a questionnaire sent to all complainants. A 'user satisfaction' survey was published in 1996.)

BIOA member?

Yes.

Funding

Funded by subscription from members. They pay a flat fee, based on the number of units managed by each member landlord.

Costs

Running cost (under the old scheme)

£509,155 in 1995/96 (£428,793 in 1994/95). The budget for the new scheme is £988,000.

Cost per complaint (under the old scheme)

Not broken down.

Staffing

Overall responsibility

The scheme secretary.

Staff

6 (all have legal, housing management or case-work qualifications). External investigators are drawn from a panel (appointed by public advertisement and interview, and supervised by the scheme secretary). External arbitrators are appointed from a panel assembled for the purpose by the Chartered Institute of Arbitrators. There are also 3 administrative staff.

Forthcoming changes

The scheme has just become statutory and will evolve, for example by the possible inclusion of private sector landlords as voluntary members.

Improving best practice

No specific powers, but the Ombudsman has an informal relationship with a group of housing association executives to discuss complaints issues. The Ombudsman highlights areas of difficulty in the *Annual Report* (for example, standards of leasehold management) and publishes the scheme's own research.

Facts and figures

New complaints received (including ineligible and telephone complaints)

Subject of complaint	1994/95	1995/96	% change
Disrepair	275	297	8
Nuisance/harassment	156	198	27
Transfers/allocations	219	182	-17
Service charges	104	115	10
Rent	109	57	-48
Consultation/communication	67	47	-30
Other	110	144	31

Complaints at each stage in the procedure[1]

	1994/95	1995/96	% change
Total complaints handled	1,040	1,040	-
Complaints sent back to internal procedures	811	681	-16.0
Complaints not within remit/referred elsewhere	236	240	1.5
Complaints not pursued for other reasons	N/A	135	-
Complaints for consideration	116	235	102.0
Cases resolved by Ombudsman (rather than by external arbitrators/mediators)	38	117	334.0

Outcome of complaints resolved by scheme intervention

Complaint upheld (finding of maladministration)	[1]	20 (26.5%)	-
Complaint not upheld (no maladministration)	19	56 (73.5%)	-
Resolution without formal finding	72	41	-43.0

[1] Note that not all figures are available because of reporting changes in this period.

Information available about the scheme

Publicising the scheme

As a condition of membership, landlords must publicise the scheme in their complaints procedures.

Leaflets and posters are distributed to a wide range of organisations. The new scheme is being publicised widely.

Terms of reference

These are available from the Ombudsman.

Annual Report

Published, for the old scheme, in June or July. In addition to the tables above, included analyses of casework, nature and origin of complaints, time taken, financial accounts, detailed equal opportunities classifications and analyses of complainants. The first *Annual Report* for the new scheme will be published in the summer of 1998.

Other publications

The following were published by the former Housing Association Tenants Ombudsman scheme:

Rachel Lickiss with Philip Giddings, Roy Gregory and Valerie Karn, *Research report No. 2 Setting up the Housing Association Tenants Ombudsman Service: the debate and the outcome*, 1996.

USER Research Ltd, *Research report No. 3 The Handling of Complaints: tenants' and housing associations' views*, 1996.

Research International Ltd, *Research report No. 4 Why Are There Disparities in the Level of Complaints?*, 1996.

Rachel Lickiss and Manchester University, *Research report No. 1 Housing Association Complaints Procedures*, 1995.

The old scheme also published guidance notes for organisations covered by the scheme and an annual digest of cases.

The Housing Association Ombudsman for Scotland

Drumsheugh Toll, 2 Belford Road, Edinburgh EH4 3BL
Tel: 0131 220 0599. Fax: 0131 220 0577

Ombudsman: John Richards

1. Using the scheme: key points

Service-providers covered

All housing associations and co-operatives registered with Scottish Homes.

Other non-public sector landlords who voluntarily apply to be bound by the Ombudsman's authority and who are accepted by him as participating landlords.

Complaints covered

Complaints of personal injustice as a consequence of maladministration by, or on behalf of, landlords within the Ombudsman's jurisdiction. Typically, these are complaints about:

- applications for and allocations of homes;
- repairs and improvements;
- the handling of neighbour disputes by associations;
- shared ownership rights;
- home loss/disturbance payments;
- the handling of rent and service charges (but not the charges themselves);
- problems with arrangements for relocating people while work is done to their homes.

Complaints not covered

Commercial decisions.

The level or amount of rents and service charges.

Neighbour disputes.

Complaints against Scottish Homes and other public sector landlords.

Complaints by owner occupiers about repair and improvement works to their properties carried out under comprehensive tenemental improvement schemes to which associations have acted as principal clients.

Complaints which are subject to court proceedings or which are about to go to court, arbitration or a tribunal.

Who can complain?

Private individuals who:

- are tenants of, or who have a shared ownership agreement with, a housing association or participating landlord;

- have a housing management service contract or other service agreement with a housing association or participating landlord;

- are applicants for a tenancy with one of the member bodies.

Cost

Free to complainants.

Geographical limits

The complaint must relate to the activities of housing associations and other member landlords in properties in Scotland.

Time limits

The Ombudsman will not normally accept for investigation a complaint about events known to the complainant more than 12 months before they are brought to the notice of the housing association or the Ombudsman.

Remedies

Financial compensation

There is no maximum amount that can be awarded as compensation, recompense or restitution. The Ombudsman can recommend payments for time and trouble as well as actual financial loss. The basis of the recommendation as well as the recommendation itself, is at the Ombudsman's discretion.

Other

The Ombudsman can recommend a reversal or amendment to a decision, or making an apology.

2. The complaints procedure

Making a complaint

There is a leaflet about the scheme with a tear-off complaints form (which is not compulsory). Complaints must normally be in writing but in special circumstances complaints can be dictated over the telephone (for example, if someone cannot read or write). Cassettes have been used to communicate with a blind complainant.

Exhausting the internal complaints procedure

The Ombudsman does not look into a complaint unless it has first been made to the association or participating landlord, and will not usually pursue it until it has first exhausted the landlord's internal complaints procedure. Depending on the circumstances, the complainant will be asked to follow the landlord's internal complaints procedure or the Ombudsman will ask the landlord to help the complainant use the internal procedure.

If the landlord's procedure is inadequate, or if the complaint has been dealt with too slowly, the Ombudsman may decide to take up the case.

Powers of investigation

Associations registered with Scottish Homes are expected to co-operate with enquiries. Other participating landlords undertake to do so as a condition of acceptance into the scheme.

Criteria for decisions

Statutory duties and common law.

Contracts and agreements made between landlord and tenant.

The association's or landlord's published policies.

Good practice, especially as indicated by guidance issued by Scottish Homes and the Scottish Federation of Housing Associations.

Confidentiality

The Ombudsman acts with discretion in deciding whether to send copies of correspondence from one party to the other party, or to summarise or quote from all or parts of correspondence. A complainant's letters are not normally copied to the housing association but are usually summarised. Copies of supporting documents may be sent. Copies of letters from housing associations are frequently sent to the complainant. Associations are expected to maintain confidentiality.

The Ombudsman's reports of formal investigations, apart from identifying the landlord concerned, do not mention the name of any person, or contain any particulars which are likely to identify any person. The reports go to the complainant and to the association or landlord concerned. The reports are normally made available in full to anyone who asks for them. In exceptional circumstances (for example, if publication of the full report would put an unnamed complainant at risk), the Ombudsman would publish a summary of his findings only.

Stages in complaint resolution

Assessment

The Ombudsman first decides if the complaint is within his authority and if internal complaints procedures have been exhausted. In 1995/96, out of a total of 131 cases considered, 26 were found to be outside the Ombudsman's authority; 24 were not proceeded with by the complainant; and 8 were procedurally ineligible for various reasons, including the availability of alternative means of resolution. 14 were referred back to be dealt with under the association's internal complaints procedure or were still being dealt with at the year end. No evidence of maladministration was found in 36 cases.

Acceptance and inquiries

Once a complaint is accepted, the Ombudsman will contact the landlord for more information. Where possible, the Ombudsman will encourage the parties to reach an informal settlement without need of a formal investigation.

Formal investigation

If an informal settlement is unlikely or cannot be agreed, the Ombudsman may investigate and issue a report. The report, which may include recommendations, is normally published.

Progress reports

Complainants are informed of all correspondence with the landlord and deadlines for response. The complainant is given regular updates throughout the process.

Types of ruling

Informal settlement

In 1995/96, 21 cases were resolved informally to the satisfaction of the complainants.

Formal recommendation and report

In 1995/96, 2 cases were the subject of formal investigations. In both cases findings of maladministration led to recommendations for redress.

Rights of appeal against a decision

There is no right of appeal against a decision by the Ombudsman. No decision by the Ombudsman prevents a complainant or landlord from taking proceedings in the courts or seeking arbitration.

It is not established whether the scheme is subject to judicial review.

Failure to comply with rulings

The Ombudsman cannot enforce compliance with his recommendations but Scottish Homes expects compliance. All formal recommendations made to date have been complied with by associations.

How long does the process take?

Target timescale

Initial decision on complaint - 6 weeks. Formal investigation - 6 months from commencement of formal investigation.

Actual timescale

Initial decision on the complaint - about 6 weeks (more than the previous year). Formal investigation - about 6 months from commencement of formal investigation (less than the previous year). Target timescales are achieved in 95% of cases.

Delegation of decision-making

The Ombudsman makes all decisions, such as whether there is maladministration. Notification of whether a case falls outside the scheme's remit is given by the investigator.

Following up complaints

Complainants sent back to internal complaints procedures are contacted by the investigator. If they do not respond, the investigator will normally contact the landlord to check if a complaint was received.

Complaining about the scheme itself

The scheme has its own internal complaints procedure. If someone wants to complain about administrative errors or failures in the service, the Ombudsman personally investigates how the complaint was handled and gives a detailed response. If he considers that the service mishandled the case, he will take such action as is necessary to put matters right and will review the service's procedures to ensure the failure does not happen again.

If the complainant remains dissatisfied, he/she may write to the chief executive of Scottish Homes, who will write giving his conclusions.

If the complainant is unhappy about the way in which Scottish Homes has handled the complaint, his/her MP can take up the case with the Parliamentary Ombudsman (see separate entry on page 69).

3. The scheme's structure and administration

Origins and membership

The scheme was set up in April 1994.

Structure and accountability

The scheme has no Council or Board. The Ombudsman submits a report to the Board of Scottish Homes, for information, on the general operation of the service. There is no exchange of information on individual cases between Scottish Homes and the Ombudsman service.

The Ombudsman

Appointment

Appointed by Scottish Homes. Employed part-time (1 day per week).

Monitoring

The scheme has internal time targets.

BIOA member?

No.

Funding

Funded by Scottish Homes.

Costs

Running costs in 1995/96 were £106,572.

Staffing

The Ombudsman 1 day per week, a full-time investigator and a full time personal assistant.

Forthcoming changes

None anticipated.

Improving best practice

The Ombudsman publishes, for the use of landords in the scheme, half-yearly newsletters containing summaries of recent investigations and discussion of current good practice issues.

Facts and figures

Workload 1995/96

		% change on 1994/95
Total initial complaints	131	+20
Initial complaints sent back to internal procedures; or still being dealt with at year end	14	-27
Initial complaints not pursued for other reasons	68	+26
Complaints reaching the next stage in the complaints process	47	+51
Complaints reaching the final stage in the complaints process	2	-60

Outcome of complaints fully investigated

Complaints upheld in whole or in part	2	-50
Complaint not upheld	0	-100

New complaints received 1995/96

Applications, allocations and transfers	31%
Repairs and improvements	18%
Miscellaneous	12%
Neighbour disputes	11%
Shared ownership/right to buy	7%
Home loss/disturbance payments	6%
Building or improvement contracts	5%
Rent and service charges	5%
Decant problems	3%
Tenant's incentive scheme	2%
Total	100%

Information about the scheme

Publicising the scheme

Landlords are expected to publicise the scheme.

Posters and leaflets are available in several languages. They are distributed to landlords, public libraries, and citizens advice bureaux.

Annual Report

Published in September. Gives an overview of the administrative performance of housing associations, details of casework, statistics, financial accounts etc.

Insurance Ombudsman Bureau

City Gate One, 135 Park Street, London SE1 9EA
Tel: 0171 928 4488. Inquiry Line: 0171 928 7600
Fax: 0171 401 8700/928 7678

Ombudsman: Walter Merricks

1. Using the scheme: key points

Service-providers covered

Around 96% of eligible companies, namely:

- companies authorised to carry on insurance business in the United Kingdom, Isle of Man and the Channel Islands;

- European Union companies carrying out insurance business in the UK;

- members of Lloyds insurance market.

Those not covered by the scheme include two major providers of private medical insurance.

Complaints covered

The scheme covers personal general insurance policies (eg. motor, household, travel, etc.). It does not cover life or long-term insurance, which is now covered by the Personal Investment Authority Ombudsman (see separate entry on page 177).

The scheme covers any complaint concerning a claim made under an insurance policy (provided it is the type of policy covered by the scheme).

If a member insurer fails to inform a complainant about the Insurance Ombudsman scheme, the Ombudsman can treat this as maladministration.

Complaints not covered

Disputes concerning anybody else's right to the policy money, for example third party claims.

Aspects of a policy which relate to a business or trade carried on by the complainant, unless the insurance company agrees.

Mortgage guarantee or loan protection policies for secured loans where the complainant is not specifically named as the person insured.

Complaints about the underwriting of the policy and the actuarial standards applied, including the level of premiums and decisions about which risks to cover, other than complaints of unlawful discrimination.

'Frivolous and vexatious' cases where the complainant stands no reasonable chance of success.

Complaints which are already the subject of legal proceedings or arbitration.

Who can complain?

Private individuals who are policy holders.

Friends, legal representatives and relatives on someone else's behalf.

Personal representatives, relatives and beneficiaries on behalf of a dead person.

(Not companies, partnerships or bodies such as clubs and charities.)

Cost

Free to complainants.

Geographical limits

The insurance policy must be governed by the laws of the United Kingdom, Isle of Man or Channel Isles.

The complainant must ordinarily be resident in the UK, Isle of Man or Channel Isles, either at the time of the complaint or when the policy was taken out.

Time limits

Complaints must reach the scheme within 6 months of the insurer's final decision about the complaint.

The Ombudsman can only consider the complaint outside the time limit with the agreement of the insurer concerned.

Remedies

Financial compensation

For failure to pay a claim in whole or in part:

- Maximum binding amount: £100,000 or £20,000 a year for permanent health insurance. (Average award in 1995 was £5,400.29; highest actual award was £271,400.)

The Ombudsman can also make non-binding recommendations to pay higher amounts.

For administrative failure, including distress and inconvenience:

- Maximum binding amount: unlimited. (Typical actual award in 1996 was £250; highest actual award was £41,528.25.)

Can order the payment of interest on an award (and usually does so where he has revised a member's earlier offer in favour of the policy holder).

Can award the costs of legal or other expert advice to a complainant, eg. in the case of delay (but it is rare for an award to a policy holder to be reduced by any costs incurred by the insurer).

Can reduce the amount of an award if the complainant has contributed to the problem, for example by causing a delay.

Other

Can recommend the company makes an apology or takes corrective action, for example asking the company to rewrite misleading literature.

2. The complaints procedure

Making the complaint

Complaints must be in writing, but an oral complaint is acceptable to start the process off. There is a standard complaint form (and a guidance leaflet) but it is not essential to use it. The scheme is exploring ways of improving help for those who have difficulty completing the form.

Exhausting the internal complaints procedure

Although most complainants approach the scheme direct, the Ombudsman cannot rule on a complaint until the complainant has a letter from the insurer, signed by a senior manager, confirming that the complaint has not been settled through its internal complaints system. (Scheme staff will help complainants to follow the company's internal procedure.)

Technically, the requirement for a letter cannot be waived, but in practice the Ombudsman would treat a member which failed to provide one as having waived its rights.

Powers of investigation

Has the power to request information relating to the complaint. The Ombudsman routinely requests all company files. If an insurer refuses to provide information, the Ombudsman must report its non-compliance to the scheme's Council. The ultimate sanction would be expulsion from the scheme. The Ombudsman cannot compel an insurer to attend a hearing.

Criteria for decisions

In practice, most emphasis is placed on what is fair and reasonable in all the circumstances.

The terms of the insurance policy.

The legal position; general principles of good insurance, investment and marketing practice (including various codes of practice and regulators' rules); and any general guidance from the scheme's Council.

The Ombudsman must take into account the decisions of his predecessors, but is not bound by them.

Confidentiality

During an investigation, the complainant's statement is sent to the member company. No other documentation is sent: each party is informed of the nature of the evidence relied on by the other side, but no actual documents are exchanged.

Noteworthy cases are published in the *Annual Report* and in regular bulletins, but neither party is identified by name.

Stages in complaint resolution

Enquiries and applications

Complaints are first screened by enquiries and applications staff, to ensure they are within the scheme's jurisdiction. If the complaint is eligible, the member company is asked to provide its file. If it is not, the complainant is advised of other bodies which might be able to help.

Investigation

Eligible complaints are allocated to an executive officer, who investigates the case. Following the investigation, the executive officer sends a draft conclusion to the party against whom the scheme is likely to find. If the balance of evidence favours the complainant, it is called an advice letter and it goes to the member company; if the balance favours the company, it is called a provisional view letter and goes to the complainant. One month is given for a response.

Adjudication

The executive officer considers the response to the draft conclusion. If his or her view of the case remains the same and the draft conclusion is not accepted by the party concerned, the file is put to a senior executive or the Deputy Ombudsman or the Ombudsman to adjudicate. An adjudication is decided on the basis of documents, unless there is a conflict of evidence which can only be resolved by a hearing (held by the Ombudsman or Deputy Ombudsman at the scheme's office).

Decision

After adjudication, a decision letter is issued. The complainant has 1 month to accept or reject the decision.

Progress reports

Complainants are notified about progress at least every 6 weeks.

Types of ruling

Mediation

77% of all cases in 1996 were resolved by case-handler mediation.

Formal decision

23% of all cases in 1996 were resolved by decision by the Ombudsman.

Rights of appeal against a decision

There is no right of appeal against a formal decision, but the Ombudsman will always consider new material that was not available at the time of his investigation.

The complainant retains the right to take the case to the courts if still dissatisfied. Member companies have no right of appeal to an external body.

The scheme is not subject to judicial review.

An issue raised by an insurer concerning the Ombudsman's jurisdiction can be referred by a formal procedure to an external arbitration - but this recourse is not available to the complainant.

Failure to comply with rulings

In the last resort, the scheme's Board would have to consider the expulsion of the insurer concerned. (In practice, there have been no failures to comply in the lifetime of the scheme.)

How long does the process take?

Target timescale

To deal with complaints within 112 calendar days (16 weeks).

Actual timescale

It took 135 calendar days (just under 20 weeks) to deal with complaints in 1996.

Delegation of decision-making

There is a Deputy Insurance Ombudsman, who is an Ombudsman - and takes decisions - in his own right. The Ombudsman reads through a minority of letters and signs even fewer.

He delegates to senior staff the power to decide on specific cases not involving new precedents or points of principle (and neither he nor the Deputy Ombudsman will hear any kind of appeal from these decisions).

Following up complaints

Cases not within the scheme's remit are not followed up (but probably around 8% of written and telephone enquiries eventually return to the scheme as eligible complaints).

The scheme checks with complainants that decisions have been complied with by insurers.

Complaining about the scheme itself

There is an internal complaints procedure. Complaints are referred to the line manager responsible for the individual about whom the complaint is brought or, if necessary, to the Ombudsman. Where a serious complaint is raised that the Ombudsman has not handled a case satisfactorily, it is referred to the chairman of the scheme's Council. The chairman cannot review the decision made, but can take a view on whether the case has been handled in accordance with normal procedures. (In 1996, 30 complaints were received about the scheme's service: 4 were upheld in full, 2 were upheld in part.)

3. The scheme's structure and administration

Origins and membership

A voluntary scheme, set up as an unlimited company not having a share capital. Started operating in 1981.

Structure and accountability

The scheme is overseen by a Council and a Board.

The Council

Membership

12 members: a maximum of 9 are appointed by the Council who represent the consumer or the public interest, and a maximum of 3 who are industry representatives appointed by the Board. The chairman is a lay member.

Role

To appoint one or more Insurance Ombudsmen and to protect their independence; to set the terms of reference in line with the scheme's memorandum of association; to oversee the finances and to approve the budget (subject to Board approval); and to receive and publish the Ombudsman's *Annual Report*. Does not discuss the merits of individual decisions, but may give 'assistance and guidance' to the Ombudsmen. Meets every two months.

The Board

Membership

Up to 12 members, all industry representatives elected by the scheme members.

Role

To approve the budget and provide the scheme's finances. Plays no part in the resolution of complaints. Meets quarterly.

The Ombudsman and Deputy Ombudsman

Appointment

By the Council. Must stand down if bankrupt or of unsound mind, or if they perform any act likely to lead them or the scheme into disrepute. Prohibited from being a company director. (The Ombudsman does not have the power to dismiss the Deputy Ombudsman.)

Terms of appointment

The Ombudsman is appointed for 3 years, reappointment is permitted for up to 7 years excluding any time as Deputy Ombudsman. The Deputy Ombudsman is appointed for rolling periods of 3 years.

Roles

Running the office and handling complaints. The Deputy is an Ombudsman in his own right and the Ombudsman has no power to consider an appeal on any of his case decisions. The Ombudsman does determine the extent to which a Deputy Ombudsman exercises his jurisdiction and functions.

Scheme's terms of reference

These are set - and can be changed - by the Council, provided they remain within the objectives of the scheme as set out in the memorandum and articles of association. The overall scope of the scheme can be changed by the Board.

Monitoring

Standards of service are published in the *Annual Report*.

In the past, the scheme has allowed independent researchers to investigate complainants' satisfaction with its service (see Other publications below). In 1996 the scheme itself assessed complainants' satisfaction with a 'call management system' (a tape-recorded helpline). A stakeholder satisfaction survey project is also under way.

BIOA member?

Yes.

Funding

Comes from the members: 75% of running costs are met by a case fee, 25% by a general levy.

Costs

Running cost

£3.9 million in 1996 (£3.6 million in 1995).

Cost per complaint

£642 in 1996. (Overall costs decreased with the transfer at the end of 1996 of financial services complaints to the Personal Investment Authority Ombudsman: this may increase unit costs.)

Staffing

Overall responsibility

The Ombudsman.

Staff

Approximately 50 full-time equivalents (3 senior executives, 20 executives dealing with general insurance cases (about half come from the insurance industry, half are lawyers), 7 enquiries and applications staff and 20 support staff).

Forthcoming changes

At the end of 1996 all life and long-term insurance complaints formerly within the jurisdiction of the Insurance Ombudsman scheme moved to the Personal Investment Authority scheme. A quality assurance programme is under way addressing all aspects of the scheme's performance.

Improving best practice

Achieved through the *Annual Report* and a quarterly bulletin. A digest of Ombudsmen decisions has been published jointly with the Chartered Insurance Institute. There have been special meetings with representatives of insurers and consumer groups.

Facts and figures

Numbers of complaints completed

Subject of complaint	1995	1996	% change
Motor insurance	959	796	-7
Household insurance - contents and all-risk	766	592	-23
Household insurance - buildings	656	568	-13
Personal accident/sickness/loan protection insurance	697	422	-39
Travel insurance	354	293	-17
Permanent health insurance	194	183	-6
Medical expenses	76	91	20
Legal expenses	66	51	-14
Builders' guarantee insurance	48	48	0
Miscellaneous	42	111	164
Caravan insurance	29	11	-62
Marine insurance	27	15	-44
Livestock insurance	24	18	-25
Financial services disputes			
Pensions	638	724	12
Unit trusts	6	12	100
Industrial life insurance	13	20	53
Other life insurance	1,944	2,003	3

Numbers of complaints at each stage of procedure

	1995	1996	% change
Enquiries (written and telephone) sent back to internal complaints procedures	20,249	31,774	57
Enquiries (written and telephone) not within remit/referred elsewhere	27,015	34,642	28
Total complaints closed	6,539	6,074	-7
Complaints settled by casehandler	4,970	4,676	-6
Complaints determined by the Ombudsmen	1,569	1,397	-11

Outcome

	1995	1996	% change
Complaints not pursued	392 (6%)	374 (6%)	-5
Complaint upheld	2,289 (35%)	2,104 (35%)	-
Complaint not upheld	3,856 (59%)	3,495 (59%)	-

Information available about the scheme

Publicising the scheme

It is a condition of membership that companies inform their policy holders about the scheme's existence.

Scheme leaflets are issued to members (for distribution to policy holders) and to bodies such as citizens advice bureaux and trading standards departments.

Terms of reference

Published in the *Annual Report*.

Annual Report

Usually published in February. In addition to the tables above, includes: historic information on the number of enquiries and cases; a more detailed breakdown of cases, by subject, by cause of complaint, and by outcome; and analyses of enquiries outside the terms of reference.

Other publications

Insurance Ombudsman Bureau, *A Digest of Annual Reports and Bulletins 1981 - 1995*, 1996.

S. Rees, 'One Ombudsman too many', *Post Magazine*, Vol. 155, No. 9, 3 March 1994.

N. Munro, 'The Insurance Ombudsman Bureau and Financial Services Disputes - an obituary?', *Journal of Financial Regulation and Compliance*, Vol. 2, No. 3, 1994.

R. Gordon and S. Gordzinski, 'Insuring against judicial review', *New Law Journal*, Vol. 144, No. 6632, 21 January 1994.

A. McGee, 'Challenging decisions of the Insurance Ombudsman', *Tolley's Insurance Law and Practice,* Vol. 4, No. 2, 1994.

National Consumer Council, *Ombudsman Services: Consumers' Views of the Office of the Building Societies Ombudsman and the Insurance Ombudsman Bureau*, 1993.

Insurance Ombudsman Bureau, *Guide for applicants,* 1993.

J. Birds and C. Graham, *Complaints against insurance companies*, 1992.

J. Farrand, *The pros and cons of the private ombudsman,* Chartered Insurance Institute Society of Fellows, 1992.

A. McGee, *The Financial Services Ombudsmen* 1992.

Insurance Ombudsman Bureau, *How the Insurance Ombudsman Can Help You,* 1991.

Also publishes quarterly bulletins; digest of cases (with the Chartered Insurance Institute).

Insurance Ombudsman of Ireland

32 Upper Merrion Street, Dublin 2
Tel: 00 3531 662 0899. Fax: 00 3531 662 0890
E-mail: enquiries@ombudsman-insurance.ie

Ombudsman: Paulyn Marrinan Quinn

1. Using the scheme: key points

Service-providers covered

99% of Ireland's life and non-life insurance companies.

Complaints covered

Complaints in connection with claims made under an insurance policy.

Complaints concerning the marketing or administration of a policy.

A company's failure to inform a complainant about the Ombudsman scheme.

Complaints not covered

Disputes about life insurance concerning the actuarial standards, tables and principles which the insurer applies to its business, including the method of calculation of surrender values, paid up policy values, and the bonus system and bonus rates applicable.

Complaints concerning the premium rates charged.

Disputes or questions relating to the conduct of an insurance intermediary, except intermediaries for whom the insurer bears full legal responsibility (so the acts or omissions of tied insurance agents are covered).

Complaints where the basic benefits are more than IR£100,000 (or more than IR£10,000 per year for permanent health insurance). Complaints outside the time limits for legal action (usually 6 years).

Complaints where the subject matter has, even in part, been included in a previous complaint to the Ombudsman (unless there is new evidence).

Cases already subject to court proceedings, or cases which have been referred to the courts or to arbitration and cases that have been, or can be, dealt with by the Pensions Board. The Ombudsman can also refuse to deal with a complaint if, in her opinion, it would be more appropriately dealt with by a court of law.

Who can complain?

Private individuals or their legal representatives.

The personal representatives or beneficiaries of a dead person.

Cost

Free to complainants.

Geographical limits

The insurance policy from which the complaint arises must have been taken out in the Republic of Ireland.

Time limits

Complaints must be referred to the Ombudsman within 6 months of the complainant receiving written confirmation from the insurance company that the dispute has not been settled.

If the company has failed to tell the complainant about his/her right to use the scheme, the Ombudsman may decide to deal with the case outside the time limit.

Remedies

Financial compensation

A financial award is only made for actual financial loss. Maximum award: IR£100,000 (or IR£10,000 per year for permanent health insurance policies). The award is often made through reinstatement of the policy or payment of benefits due.

Can order the payment of interest on awards.

Cannot usually award the costs of legal or other expert advice, but may ask the company to pay for (a) expert reports - such as a medical report - it has insisted upon and/or (b) reasonable legal costs incurred as a result of a company's failure to inform the complainant of the right to go to the Ombudsman.

May reduce the amount awarded if the complainant's own actions contributed to the problem.

Other

The Ombudsman can recommend corrective action, for example the return of premiums or reinstatement of a policy. She can also recommend that the company makes an apology.

2. The complaints procedure

Making the complaint

Complaints must eventually be in writing, although an oral complaint is acceptable to start off the process. A standard complaint form and a guidance leaflet are available, including braille, audio cassette and computer disk versions for people who have difficulty completing the form. Staff will also take verbal instructions.

Exhausting the internal complaints procedure

Before the Ombudsman can start investigating, complainants must first have exhausted all internal channels of complaint within the member company. The company must issue a 'signing-off' letter (signed by a senior executive), confirming that the case has not been settled to the complainant's satisfaction.

If the company has failed to respond to a complainant within 2 months of first receiving the complaint in writing, the Ombudsman can decide to deal with the complaint without the signing-off letter.

In special circumstances the Ombudsman may be able to help, through mediation, before the internal complaints system has been exhausted.

Powers of investigation

Has powers to request information from member companies concerning a complaint. (Refusal to supply information would be referred to the scheme's Board.)

Criteria for decisions

The terms of the insurance contract.

Relevant legal principles and general principles of good insurance practice (including the Irish Insurance Federation's codes of practice).

The Ombudsman's previous decisions are taken into account to a certain degree, but each case is decided on its merits.

What is fair and reasonable. In practice, most emphasis is placed on arriving at a fair and reasonable outcome.

Confidentiality

Documents are not routinely copied to the other side during investigations, except with specific permission.

Anonymous case studies - without names and only identifying the type of insurance institution concerned - are published in the *Annual Report*.

Stages in complaint resolution

Preliminary stage

Complainants who have not yet exhausted the internal complaints procedure are sent the explanatory leaflet and guide for complainants, and directed back to a nominated member of senior management within the insurance company.

If the case is not within the scheme's remit, staff will give guidance on other possible ports of call or, where appropriate, forward the complaint automatically.

Investigation

When a completed complaints form is received, if it is within the scheme's terms of reference, the Ombudsman writes to the insurance company requesting their comments, the case file and supporting documents. Once the Ombudsman receives the case file, she may ask the complainant for further information, and conduct further investigations or research. Where necessary, if there is a conflict of evidence on the facts, oral hearings are sometimes held at the Ombudsman's office.

At this stage, the Ombudsman may decline to handle the case, either because it is not eligible under the terms of reference or because she believes it would be more appropriately dealt with by the courts. In other cases, the Ombudsman may be able to suggest ways of settling the dispute informally. If the company decides to make an 'ex-gratia' offer, the Ombudsman expects the offer to be made through her so that she can discuss it with the complainant.

Pre-decision opinion

In more complex cases, the Ombudsman sends the parties involved a pre-decision opinion letter, setting out the view she has formed. The complainant and company then have an opportunity to produce any further evidence in support of their argument.

Adjudication

Unless there is compelling new evidence, the Ombudsman will confirm her pre-decision opinion in an adjudication. If she makes an award which is accepted by the complainant, she asks the complainant for written confirmation that the award is accepted in full and final settlement of the claim. Once this is received, it is sent on to the insurance company - which, in the case of a financial award, issues a cheque directly to the complainant.

Progress reports

Complainants are informed as each stage is reached and also get 'keep in touch' letters.

Types of ruling

Informal conciliation

Just under 50% of resolved cases are settled in this way.

Adjudication

This is binding on the member company, but not on the complainant. Just over 50% of resolved cases are settled through adjudication.

Rights of appeal against a decision

A case can only be re-opened if new evidence comes to light that was not available at the outset.

The complainant always keeps his/her right to take the case to court.

It is not yet established whether the scheme is subject to judicial review.

Failure to comply with rulings

The company would be reported to the scheme's Board via the Council. (In practice, there have been no cases of non-compliance.) Ultimately the company could be expelled from the scheme.

How long does the process take?

Target timescale

For dealing with complaints - 6 to 9 months.

Actual timescale

For dealing with complaints - this depends on the complexity of the case.

In urgent cases the Ombudsman may sometimes intervene before the case has been 'signed-off' by the insurance company.

Delegation of decision-making

> There is no Deputy Ombudsman or equivalent, and the Ombudsman's powers are not delegated in any way. She signs every decision letter.

Following up complaints

> Where the complaint is not within the scheme's jurisdiction or the complainant has not exhausted an internal complaints procedure, the complainant is asked to provide feedback.

> The Ombudsman asks for confirmation from both parties that decisions have been complied with.

> The Ombudsman routinely reviews written feedback from complainants. Further research is planned.

Complaining about the scheme itself

> Complaints are referred to the scheme's Council.

3. The scheme's structure and administration

Origins and membership

> Started operating 8 October 1992. A voluntary scheme, set up as a company limited by guarantee.

Structure and accountability

> The scheme is overseen by a Council and a Board.

The Council

Membership

> 7 members, including 2 (at most) industry nominees. The chairman is a lay member. The first members were appointed by the Board; on retirement they are now replaced by co-option.

Role

> To appoint the Ombudsman, to safeguard her independence and to ensure that she is

adequately resourced. Receives a proposed budget from the Ombudsman and recommends it to the Board when approved. Monitors the terms of reference. Plays no part in the resolution of complaints. Meets quarterly.

The Board

Membership

Currently 8, all from the insurance industry and elected by member companies.

Role

To provide funds for the scheme. Plays no part in the resolution of complaints. Meets quarterly.

The Ombudsman

Appointment

By the Council. Can only be dismissed for misconduct or on absence through illness.

Term of appointment

Maximum initial term: 2 years. Reappointment permitted for a second term of 3 years.

Role

Responsible for running the office and complaints-handling.

Scheme's terms of reference

Laid down in a separate document when the scheme was established. Can be changed by the Board, on the recommendation of the Council and in consultation with the Ombudsman.

Monitoring

Service standards are published in the *Annual Report*.

BIOA member?

Yes.

Funding

Funding comes from the member companies - they pay a levy representing a flat fee of premium income.

Costs

Running cost

IR£235,000 in 1995 (an increase from IR£190,000 in 1994).

Cost per complaint

Not analysed.

Staffing

Overall responsibility

The Ombudsman has overall responsibility for running the office.

Staff

There is an office administrator, 4 support staff, 2 full-time and 2 part-time case researchers/ reporters. Staff usually have legal and/or insurance backgrounds.

Forthcoming changes

None.

Improving best practice

The use of 'best practice' as a criterion for arriving at a decision itself raises standards. The Ombudsman also has informal links with the Irish Insurance Federation and with the relevant Minister at the Department for Enterprise and Employment.

Facts and figures

New complaints received in writing (including ineligible complaints)

Subject of complaint	1995	1996	% change
Life	229	105	-54.0
Investment	92	120	30.0
Educational	14	10	-40.0
Motor	154	100	-54.0
Household buildings	34	48	37.0
Household contents	33	18	-45.0
Travel	33	22	-33.0
Mortgage/loan protection	40	52	30.0
Permanent health/personal accident/income continuance/salary protection	58	47	-19.0
Pension	39	37	-5.0
Commercial	16	14	-12.5
General	54	23	-57.0
Medical expenses	29	39	34.5

Numbers of complaints at each stage of procedure

	1995	1996	% change
Written complaints received	825	635	-23.0
Complaints outside terms of reference	240	159	-34.0
Complaints where jurisdiction declined (court action already instituted/more appropriate)	37	31	-16.0
Complaints closed/lapsed	126	111	-12.0
Cases settled	172	175	2.0
Cases adjudicated	151	186	23.0

Outcome of adjudications

	1995	1996	
Favourable to complainant	63 (42%)	89 (48%)	-
Favourable to company	84 (56%)	97 (52%)	-
No ruling (evidential difficulties or allegations of fraud made case more suitable for court action)	4 (2%)	0 (0%)	-

Information available about the scheme

Publicising the scheme

The Ombudsman takes the view that insurance companies have an obligation to inform complainants of the existence of the scheme.

A scheme leaflet and guidance for complainants are widely distributed.

The Ombudsman also undertakes speaking engagements, gives lectures to law and business studies faculties and is working to produce a quarterly digest of cases.

Terms of reference

These are published in some *Annual Reports* and available on request.

Annual Report

Usually published March. Includes detailed breakdowns of complaints outside jurisdiction, the reasons for complaints, and the outcome of complaints by type of policy, plus information on time taken to resolve complaints.

Other publications

M. Cousins, 'Personal insurance policies - definitions of disability', *Commercial Law Practitioner*, October 1994.

Also publishes guidance notes for organisations covered by the scheme.

Office of the Investment Ombudsman

6 Frederick's Place, London EC2R 8BT
Tel: 0171 796 3065. Fax: 0171 726 0574

Ombudsman: Peter Dean

1. Using the scheme: key points

Service-providers covered

Investment managers, unit trust managers and pension fund managers - if their business is regulated by IMRO (the Investment Management Regulatory Organisation). (Not all investment businesses are regulated by IMRO.)

Complaints covered

Complaints about financial loss, distress and inconvenience in connection with personal investments like pensions, personal equity plans (PEPs), unit trusts and investment trusts.

Complaints not covered

Complaints about a fall in the value of an investment caused solely by movements in the market.

Cases involving the management of a private family trust.

Problems that arose before 30 April 1988 or before the investment business in question became authorised under the Financial Services Act.

Complaints on which a court has already ruled. Complainants and scheme members usually have to agree they will not take any other action, including going to court, while the complaint is with the Ombudsman.

Who can complain?

Private individuals, groups of individuals, businesses, charities and other unincorporated bodies.

Friends, relatives and legal representatives of living individuals, so long as the Ombudsman is satisfied that the person cannot complain personally, for instance because of ill health.

The representatives of a dead person.

Cost

Free to complainants.

Geographical limits

UK-wide, so long as the body complained about is regulated by IMRO.

Time limits

Complaints must reach the scheme, in writing, within 3 years of the date on which the complainant knew (or ought to have known) of the events that gave rise to the problem.

The Ombudsman can accept a complaint outside this time limit if he is satisfied it was not reasonably practicable for the complainant to refer it earlier, provided it then reaches him within a reasonable time.

Remedies

Financial compensation

Maximum possible award for financial loss is £100,000 (actual maximum paid in 1996/97 was £66,670).

Maximum possible award for distress and inconvenience is £750 (actual maximum in 1996/97 was £750).

If a case is upheld during adjudication, the adjudicator can invite the scheme member to pay more than the £100,000 maximum (see Stages in complaints resolution below).

Can order the payment of interest on awards where an investor has been deprived of the use of his or her funds.

Cannot award the costs of legal or other expert advice against either party.

Can, but rarely does, reduce the amount of an award if the complainant's actions contributed to the problem.

Other

Can suggest corrective action such as recommending that the company reinstate a complainant's investment portfolio as it should have been but for the investment business's actions.

Can recommend that the company issues an apology.

2. The complaints procedure

Making the complaint

Complaints must be in writing, using the scheme's standard complaints form. A guidance booklet is available and staff can give help over the telephone to those with any difficulty completing the form.

Exhausting the internal complaints procedure

Complainants can approach the scheme direct at any time. However, before the scheme investigates a complaint, the business concerned must have been given at least 2 months to resolve it. This requirement can only be waived with the agreement of the business. Once 2 months have passed and the complaint has not been resolved, the scheme can investigate.

Powers of investigation

Members of the scheme must (under IMRO rules) co-operate with the Ombudsman.

Criteria for decisions

Legal principles, subject to seeking a fair and reasonable settlement.

The scheme's previous decisions are not binding, but may give helpful guidance.

If a complaint reaches the stage of binding adjudication, the adjudicator can only make a final award if he or she is satisfied there has been a breach of a legal obligation owed to the complainant and one which would entitle the complainant to a legal remedy.

Confidentiality

During an investigation, both parties are provided with copies of the key evidence.

Detailed case reports are not published but the facts may be summarised, on a no-names basis, in the *Annual Report*.

Stages in complaint resolution

Preliminary stage

Staff will try to assess from the initial phone call whether the complaint is within the Ombudsman's jurisdiction. If it is within jurisdiction, the caller is sent a complaint form and booklet.

If a complaint is not within jurisdiction, staff try to redirect the complaint to an organisation that may be able to help.

Collecting evidence

Staff assess the completed complaint form to make sure the complaint is eligible for the scheme. If it is, the company concerned is asked for its response to the complaint and copies of the relevant papers. Evidence is collected by one of the investigative staff, mainly by letter, occasionally in interviews.

The Ombudsman's recommendation

Once all the evidence has been collated, the Ombudsman reviews the file. If there is a direct conflict of evidence, he may hold interviews either at the scheme's office or in the complainant's home. He then makes a recommendation (which is not binding on either party).

Adjudication

If either party does not accept the recommendation, the Ombudsman can decide to offer binding adjudication. This is an informal arbitration process. The adjudicator is appointed from an external panel. The adjudicator will tell the complainant the procedure to be used (for instance, whether he/she needs further evidence and whether by correspondence or an informal hearing. The Ombudsman can, if requested, help a complainant to present the case to the adjudicator.

Final award

The adjudicator can make a binding final award. However, an adjudication can be cancelled (and would no longer be binding) if the adjudicator decides that

- the company ought to pay the complainant more than the scheme's £100,000 maximum; or

- the company has a justified case against the complainant and the complainant owes money to the company. If the party concerned refuses to make the payment, the adjudication is cancelled and the case can be referred to the courts.

Progress reports

There is no fixed procedure but complainants are regularly informed about progress.

Types of ruling

Recommendation (by the Ombudsman)

Neither party is bound to comply (although the majority of complaints are resolved at this stage).

Adjudication (by an external adjudicator)

This is binding on both parties unless it is cancelled for the reasons above. (It has only been used 7 times since the scheme started.)

Rights of appeal against a decision

If either party is dissatisfied with the Ombudsman's recommendation they can ask for binding adjudication, although it is entirely up to the Ombudsman whether it is granted.

If a case does not go to adjudication but the complainant remains dissatisfied, he or she can still take the case to court.

If a case does go to adjudication, either party has the legal right to ask the High Court to hear an appeal, but only on a point of law.

It has not been established if the scheme is subject to judicial review.

Failure to comply with rulings

Failure to comply with Ombudsman's recommendation

The Ombudsman has no power to enforce compliance. (In practice, there has been no failure to comply with a recommendation.)

Failure to comply with an adjudication decision

The decision is enforceable in the courts under the Arbitration Acts.

How long does the process take?

Target timescale

None at present.

Actual timescale

Around 15 weeks to complete a case in 1995/96. (This average excludes 18 cases that took over 18 months to resolve, 3 that took over 20 months, and 1 - involving an adjudication - that took nearly 2 years.)

Delegation of decision-making

The Ombudsman's powers are not delegated in any way.

Following up complaints

Complaints not within the scheme's jurisdiction or where the internal complaints procedure has not been exhausted are not followed up.

Where the Ombudsman has made a recommendation, the case file is not closed until any recommended payment has been made.

Complaining about the scheme itself

If there is a complaint, the file is reviewed by the scheme's Committee. (There have been 2 complaints in the scheme's lifetime: neither was upheld.)

3. The scheme's structure and administration

Origins and membership

Started operating on 1 May 1989. The Financial Services Act 1986 requires self-regulatory bodies for financial services businesses to have a complaints-handling mechanism. The Office of the Investment Ombudsman is the complaints-handling scheme set up by IMRO. Membership of the Ombudsman scheme is a requirement of IMRO's rules. Not all investment businesses belong to IMRO.

Structure and accountability

The scheme consists of an Ombudsman and a Committee.

The Committee

Membership

3 lay members (including the chairman), 2 industry representatives. All are appointed by the board of IMRO.

Role

To oversee the scheme and ensure its independence from IMRO; to satisfy itself that the

Ombudsman has established and maintains effective arrangements for investigating complaints against IMRO members; to appoint the Ombudsman and fix his remuneration (subject to the overall policy of the IMRO board). Has no direction or influence over the investigation of complaints. Also ensures that IMRO has no direction or influence. Meets a few times a year, as necessary.

The Ombudsman

Appointment

By the Committee. Can only be dismissed if he is in breach of his contract of employment.

Term of appointment

Initially 3 years. No limits on reappointment.

Role

Overall responsibility for running the office and complaints-handling.

The scheme's terms of reference

These are set out in the Investment Ombudsman Memorandum. Can be changed by IMRO.

Monitoring

Standards of service are not published.

BIOA member?

Yes.

Funding

Comes directly from IMRO.

Costs

Running cost

£387,750 in 1996/97.

Cost per complaint

Not broken down.

Staffing

Overall responsibility

The Ombudsman.

Staff

1 executive director, 1 assistant director and 1 investigating officer (all legally qualified) and 2 administrative staff. A panel of external senior lawyers retired from private practice is available for adjudication.

Forthcoming changes

Internal procedures are to be developed but the scheme itself will remain the same. The scheme is subject to the reorganisation of financial services regulation announced by the government in May 1997.

Improving best practice

Member companies are informed when the Ombudsman feels they have not acted in accordance with best practice. Recommendations to both members and investors are made in the *Annual Report*. The scheme does not have a role in policing the investment industry.

Facts and figures

Numbers of new complaints received in writing

Subject of complaint	1994/95	1995/96	% change
Portfolio management	16	87	[1]
Pensions	0	18	[1]
PEPs	21	84	[1]
Unit trusts	5	46	[1]
Investment trusts	47	154	[1]
Other	0	26	[1]

[1] Percentage changes are not meaningful because of the closure of the IMRO complaints department, which previously dealt with some complaints.

Numbers of complaints at each stage of procedure

	1994/95	1995/96	% change
Total complaints handled	91	373	[1]
Complaints resolved	65	185	[1]

Outcome of complaints resolved

	1994/95	1995/96	% change
Complaint upheld	15 (30%)	67 (56%)	-
Complaint not upheld	35 (70%)	53 (44%)	-
Complaint taken to adjudication	0	1	-
Other outcome (eg. complaint withdrawn or settled)	15	73	-

[1] Percentage changes are not meaningful because of the closure of the IMRO complaints department, which previously dealt with some complaints.

Information available about the scheme

Publicising the scheme

A booklet about the scheme is distributed to libraries and citizens advice bureaux on request. It includes an informal guide to the scheme and the Investment Ombudsman Memorandum.

Annual Report

Published in June.

Personal Investment Authority Ombudsman Bureau

Hertsmere House, Hertsmere Road, London E14 4AB
Tel: 0171 216 0016. Fax: 0171 712 8742

Principal Ombudsman: Tony Holland
Ombudsmen: Richard Prior, Maralyn Thomas

1. Using the scheme: key points

All independent financial advisers and investment companies providing long-term insurance investments (such as life and personal pension policies) and other personal investments (such as unit trusts, and Personal Equity Plans (PEPs) and shares) which are members of the Personal Investment Authority (PIA) must belong to this scheme. There are two aspects to the scheme: the mandatory jurisdiction which covers all firms and the voluntary jurisdiction which covers most but not all firms. Whenever there are differences likely to affect complainants, we give details of both - using the captions Mandatory jurisdiction and Voluntary jurisdiction.

Service-providers covered

The mandatory jurisdiction

Almost all companies that were members of the two regulatory bodies whose functions have now been taken over by the PIA - the Life Insurance and Unit Trust Regulatory Organisation (LAUTRO) and the Financial Intermediaries, Investment Managers and Brokers Regulatory Association (FIMBRA).

FIMBRA members (or ex-FIMBRA members who are not members of the PIA, providing they did not resign from FIMBRA before 1 April 1996) providing the complaint was not referred to the FIMBRA arbitration scheme before 1 April 1996.

The PIA Ombudsman Bureau also deals with complaints against the UK's largest insurer, the Prudential, which has opted to be regulated by the

Securities and Investment Board (SIB) rather than the PIA.

The voluntary jurisdiction

Any firm that agrees to accept the voluntary jurisdiction. In practice, this means life insurance companies as the voluntary jurisdiction was established to enable life offices to adopt a scheme which mirrors the Insurance Ombudsman Bureau and to resign from that body. Consequently independent financial advisers, large or small, will not normally join.

Complaints covered

The mandatory jurisdiction

Complaints in connection with, or arising out of, investment business as defined by the Financial Services Act 1986 and regulated by the PIA - usually involving selling and marketing of investments. The products covered include life insurance; personal pensions; unit trusts; guaranteed income bonds; investment trust savings schemes; offshore funds and broker funds; portfolio management; and advice on, and arranging deals in, shares and traded options.

The voluntary jurisdiction

Complaints concerning personal investments and long-term life insurance not covered by the Financial Services Act 1986. This means it covers complaints about term insurance and permanent health insurance, and complaints about pre-Financial Services Act business and administration.

The voluntary scheme only covers complaints about investments that have been bought by, or for the benefit of, natural persons - meaning individual people, and not companies and other bodies. So, for example, a complaint about a policy taken out by, and payable to, a firm on the death of a key employee would be within the mandatory rules, but not the voluntary rules.

Complaints not covered

Most complaints about a fall in the value of an investment caused solely by market movements.

For life insurance, complaints about the actuarial standards, principles and tables on which surrender values, maturity values and the like are based.

Cases which in the Ombudsman's opinion are frivolous and vexatious (that is, those which, in the Ombudsman's view, stand no substantial chance of success).

Cases on which a court has already ruled or which are already subject to court proceedings which have not been adjourned or discontinued.

The mandatory jurisdiction

Complaints first made to the business concerned before it became a member of the PIA (but for FIMBRA member firms, see Service-providers covered above). These complaints may be dealt with by other Ombudsmen.

The voluntary jurisdiction

Complaints made to the firm before it adopted the voluntary jurisdiction.

Who can complain?

The mandatory jurisdiction

Customers of investment businesses authorised by the PIA, their widows/widowers, or any surviving dependants who have acquired an annuity or pension plan from them.

Any suitable representative (like a relative) of the customer who is either a minor or cannot act for himself/herself.

The personal representatives of a customer who has died.

Any person or body (including an incorporated body) who has acquired legal title to the investment in question other than by buying it - for example, trustees, executors and administrators.

Further, customers include people who were only potentially party to the investment agreement or service.

The voluntary jurisdiction

A person who effected the policy or contract which is the subject matter of complaint or some other person who has acquired legal title to the policy other than by buying it.

The voluntary scheme only covers complaints by natural persons whereas the mandatory jurisdiction covers complaints made by companies as well as individuals.

Cost

Free to complainants.

Geographical limits

The mandatory jurisdiction

Only covers complaints arising out of investment business in the UK. It does not however matter where the complainant lives.

The voluntary jurisdiction

The complainant must be a person whose main or principal residence is or at the time of the events giving rise to the complaint was in the UK, the Isle of Man or the Channel Islands.

Time limits

Complaints must be lodged with the Ombudsman within 6 months of reaching deadlock with the company (see Exhausting the internal complaints procedure below). The Ombudsman can decide to waive the time limit if he considers it appropriate but has indicated that he is unlikely to do so in the absence of good reasons. However, the scheme cannot deal with a complaint that would be outside the time limit for bringing that complaint to a court: broadly speaking, this is 6 years after the event from which the complaint arises or, if later, 3 years from when the complainant first appreciated (or should have appreciated) that loss or damage had been suffered.

These time limits do not apply to complaints about pension transfers and opt-outs falling within the current Securities and Investments Board review, providing the Ombudsman agrees it would be inequitable to apply the time bar.

Remedies

Financial compensation

Can make a binding award for financial loss, distress and inconvenience.

The mandatory jurisdiction

Maximum binding award for financial loss: £50,000 (£20,000 a year for permanent health insurance cases). Maximum award for distress and inconvenience: £750. (There is a proposal to increase these maximums: please see Forthcoming changes below.)

The voluntary jurisdiction

Maximum binding award for financial loss: £100,000 (£20,000 a year for permanent health insurance cases), plus an additional award of any amount for distress and inconvenience.

The highest actual award for financial loss in 1996/97 was £90,712 (the average actual award in 1995/96 was £4,120). The highest actual award for distress and inconvenience in 1996/97 was £750; the average actual award in 1995/96 was between £75 and £150. Can make a non-binding recommendation to pay compensation above the standard limits.

Can order the payment of interest on awards where complainants have been denied use of their money.

Can award the costs of the complainant's legal or expert advice, so long as it was reasonable for the complainant to seek the advice, the complaint was largely successful and the fees themselves are reasonable.

May occasionally reduce the amount of an award where the complainant has failed to take steps to reduce his or her losses.

Other

Getting an apology and corrective action. Frequently the most appropriate remedy may not be the payment of compensation but may instead be for example the re-instatement of an investment which the complainant had been incorrectly advised to surrender. The Ombudsman will make such orders whenever possible.

2. The complaints procedure

Making the complaint

Complainants can approach the scheme direct: they do not need to use an intermediary. Complaints must usually be in writing, on a standard complaints form (included in the guidance leaflet). However, a complaint over the phone is acceptable to start the process off, so long as it is followed by written confirmation. People with visual impairments can submit complaints on audio-tape, and the scheme will consider other methods where appropriate.

Exhausting the internal complaints procedure

Before the Ombudsman can deal with a complaint, the complainant must first exhaust all internal channels of complaint within the firm concerned, at senior management level. (The scheme can give advice and information to complainants about internal procedures.) The senior management of the firm must issue a 'deadlock letter', stating that the internal procedure has failed to resolve the complaint. This requirement can be waived if, in the view of the Ombudsman, the complainant has not received an adequate response within 2 months of first contacting the firm in question.

Powers of investigation

Regulated firms are obliged to co-operate with the Ombudsman and to provide any material requested.

Criteria for decisions

The law, regulatory rules, codes and guidance applicable at the time of the events which gave rise to the complaint and statements of general insurance practice. (Regulatory principles, codes and rules prevail if these are inconsistent with the law.)

The Ombudsman is not bound by his own previous decisions, although he aims for consistency.

Confidentiality

Before a decision is taken on a complaint each party is provided with copies of all relevant documents provided by the other. The Ombudsman will not normally accept evidence submitted in confidence.

Summaries of noteworthy cases are published in the *Annual Report* and PIA regulatory updates. Complainants are not identified by name, the type of institution concerned (although not individual names) is made clear.

Stages in complaint resolution

New enquiries

These are screened by the new complaints department. If the internal complaints procedure has been exhausted and the complaint appears to be within the scheme's jurisdiction, it is classified as a 'case' and allocated to a team of case officers.

If a complaint is not within the scheme's remit, the complainant is referred to any other appropriate body; where possible, complaints are automatically forwarded.

Investigation

A case officer ensures that he/she has all the necessary information. Written and occasionally visual evidence (like a video) is usually sufficient but where the evidence is inconclusive, the Ombudsman occasionally holds a face-to-face hearing (at the scheme's office).

Provisional assessment

After any necessary internal discussions, the case officer usually sends both parties a provisional assessment - that is, a letter explaining the case officer's conclusions. If the case officer feels the complaint should not succeed, the complainant will be invited to withdraw it. Otherwise, the parties are invited to settle the case by agreement, on the terms set out in the provisional assessment. Both parties have 21 days to respond (with extensions agreed, if appropriate) and the opportunity to see and comment on any relevant material.

Final decision

If the case still remains unsettled, it goes to one of the 3 Ombudsmen, who considers all the material afresh and makes a final decision.

Progress reports

Complainants are notified as each stage of the procedure is reached, and otherwise as appropriate.

Types of ruling

Informal conciliation

Used to resolve 23% of cases in 1996/97.

Non-binding recommendation

Made at the provisional assessment stage (45% of cases in 1996/97 resolved at this stage).

Final decision

This is binding on the scheme member, not on the complainant. (Decisions were issued in 14% of cases in 1996/97.)

The remaining cases received (18% in 1996/97) were either withdrawn, settled or outside the jurisdiction of the Ombudsman.

Rights of appeal against a decision

Neither side can require the Ombudsman to reconsider a decision - the Ombudsman will only do so if new evidence is produced. (There is no right of appeal from one PIA Ombudsman to another.)

Complainants who remain dissatisfied can take their case through the courts.

Member companies are legally bound to comply with the Ombudsman's decisions unless they invoke the 'test case' procedure: the member can, subject to the Ombudsman's agreement and to paying the complainant's costs, refer a case involving an important issue of principle to the courts. (No member has so far used this procedure.)

It is not yet established whether the scheme is subject to judicial review (the one application for leave to review was rejected on the merits).

Failure to comply with rulings

In practice, there have been no failures to comply with the Ombudsman's rulings.

The mandatory jurisdiction

Members are bound to comply with the Ombudsman's decisions, by the rules of the PIA.

The voluntary jurisdiction

Members are bound to comply with the Ombudsman's decisions, by their adoption of the jurisdiction.

How long does the process take?

Target timescale

6 months in 1996/97.

Actual timescale

6 months.

Cases can be given priority treatment when necessary.

Delegation of decision-making

The Ombudsman's powers to decide on complaints are not delegated in any way. The Ombudsman signs every decision letter. 1 of the 3 Ombudsmen is specifically responsible for consistency of decision-making. Complaints that are resolved before a final decision by an Ombudsman are reviewed by a team manager.

Following up complaints

The outcome of any complaint not within the remit of the scheme is not followed up.

Where cases are resolved following a provisional assessment or Ombudsman's decision, the member business provides the scheme with copy correspondence to show that the decision has been complied with.

Complaining about the scheme itself

Any complaint is initially reviewed by the scheme's general manager. If he cannot resolve it, the chairman of the scheme's Council considers whether it is serious enough to refer to a panel of the Council. (The scheme receives about 2 such complaints a month, usually about delays: about a quarter are upheld.)

3. The scheme's structure and administration

Origins and membership

The Financial Services Act 1986 requires authorised personal investment businesses to be covered by an independent complaints-handling body. This scheme - and its mandatory jurisdiction - was established by the PIA to fulfil that requirement for its members. It was set up as a company limited by guarantee and started operating for PIA members in July 1994 and commenced voluntary jurisdiction in April 1995.

Structure and accountability

There is a Board and a Council.

The Council

Membership

7 lay members (co-opted by the Council), one of whom is chairman, and 3 industry representatives (appointed by the Board).

Role

To appoint the Ombudsman; to ensure the independence of the Ombudsman; to amend the scheme's terms of reference (with Board approval); and generally to maintain awareness of the scheme's standard of service. Plays no part in the Ombudsman's decisions on individual complaints, but may discuss a case if it has led to a general point of interest or principle or if a complaint is made against the scheme itself. Meets up to 8 times per year.

The Board

Membership

The scheme's Board includes all the board members of the PIA.

Role

> To set the budget and the amount of the case fee and to appoint the scheme's general manager. Plays no part in the Ombudsman's decisions on complaints.

The three Ombudsmen

Appointment

> All 3 are appointed by the Council, which has the power of dismissal if it believes an Ombudsman is unfit for office.

Term of appointment

> Each is appointed for 3 years, with reappointment at the discretion of the Council.

Role

> 1 of the 3 is the Principal Ombudsman. All have the same powers in relation to individual complaints, but the Principal Ombudsman has ultimate authority for general principles and policy.

Scheme's terms of reference

> These are set out in the document establishing the scheme. They can be changed by the Council, with Board approval.

Monitoring

> Standards of service are published in the *Annual Report.*

> The PIA Consumer Panel conducted a postal survey of complainants to the scheme in March 1996 (it found a general level of satisfaction). The findings were summarised in *PIA Consumer Panel Report,* 1996, available from the PIA, 1 Canada Square, Canary Wharf, London E14 5AZ.

BIOA member?

> Yes.

Funding

Funding comes partly from the PIA (through a sum included in the PIA membership fee) and partly from a case fee of £500 (charged to members for each complaint received that is within jurisdiction and has exhausted the member's internal complaints procedure).

Costs

Running cost

Around £2,800,000 in 1995/96.

Cost per complaint

Not published.

Staffing

Overall responsibility

The general manager.

Staff

About 40 case officers (working in 7 teams, 1 of which concentrates on pensions); 25 staff dealing with new complaints and administration. Staff have a fairly equal spread of legal, technical and industry qualifications; no case officer who has previously worked for a member firm will deal with a complaint against that particular firm for a set period.

Forthcoming changes

The PIA has consulted on a proposal, supported by the Ombudsman, to increase the maximum awards under the mandatory jurisdiction to £100,000 and abolish the £750 limit on awards for distress and inconvenience. An increase in the former will be implemented no later than July 1998 together with an increase in the latter to £1,500.

Improving best practice

The scheme has a voluntary information-sharing agreement with the PIA. Monthly reports go to the

PIA and issues are raised as necessary. General points for the industry are raised in the *Annual Report.*

Facts and figures

<u>**Numbers of complaints received (only those within jurisdiction)**</u>

Subject of complaint	18/7/94 to 31/3/95	1995/96	% change
Breach of best advice/suitability rules	229	1,516	[1]
Misrepresentation as to nature of investment	72	639	[1]
Administration	-	132	[1]
Incorrect advice to sell and reinvest (churning)	4	116	[1]
Failure to provide information	5	72	[1]
Other conduct of business rule breach	-	69	[1]
Cases within the pensions transfers/opt outs review	-	43	[1]
Dispute over instructions	4	43	[1]
Pension premium	1	16	[1]
Negligent management	-	15	[1]
Undesirable sales conduct	-	8	[1]
General/unrelated complaint	1	8	[1]
Commission	10	7	[1]
Other	4	23	[1]

[1] Percentage changes are not meaningful as periods are of different lengths (the scheme only started in July 1994).

Number of complaints at each stage of procedure

	18/7/94 to 31/3/95	1995/96	% change
Ineligible complaint (event occurred before FSA implemented)	405	769	[1]
Ineligible complaint (not about investment business)	425	644	[1]
Ineligible complaint (not about PIA member)	270	507	[1]
Complaints ineligible for other reasons	558	1,947	[1]
Initial complaints received (potential cases where deadlock not yet reached)	1,500	7,220	[1]
New cases received	330	2,717	[1]
Cases closed	38	1,290	[1]

Outcome of cases disposed of

Resolved by provisional assessment in favour of complainant	7 [2]	270 (47%)	-
Resolved by provisional assessment in favour of scheme member	10 [2]	305 (53%)	-
Resolved by Ombudsman's decision in favour of complainant	5 [2]	126 (62%)	-
Resolved by Ombudsman's decision in favour of scheme member	1 [2]	76 (38%)	-
Cases disposed of in other ways (eg. settled, withdrawn).	9 [2]	206	-

[1] Percentage changes are not meaningful as periods are of different lengths (the scheme only started in July 1994).
[2] Numbers too small for percentages to be meaningful.

Information available about the scheme

Publicising the scheme

> The rules of the PIA require a member, within 7 business days of completing its own investigation into a complaint, to inform complainants who remain dissatisfied that they have the right to refer the complaint to the Ombudsman.

> General publicity is achieved by contacts with the press, the *Annual Report* and PIA regulatory updates. Leaflets about the scheme are held by advice agencies.

Terms of reference

Published in the *Annual Report* and available on request.

Annual Report

Usually published in May or June. As well as the tables above, gives further analyses of enquiries.

Legal Services Ombudsman for England and Wales

(The Office of the Legal Services Ombudsman)

22 Oxford Court, Oxford Street, Manchester M2 3WQ
Tel: 0161 236 9532. Fax: 0161 236 2651

Ombudsman: Michael Barnes

1. Using the scheme: key points

Service-providers covered

Lawyers who are regulated by one of the following professional bodies:

- the Office for the Supervision of Solicitors (solicitors);

- the General Council of the Bar (barristers);

- the Council for Licensed Conveyancers (lay conveyancers).

Complaints covered

Complaints about the way in which any complaint of poor service or professional misconduct has been dealt with by one of the professional bodies listed above. Most investigations do not go beyond this. However, the Ombudsman can decide to investigate the original complaint itself, when he/she considers it justified.

Complaints not covered

Complaints on which a court has already ruled or which are already subject to court proceedings.

Issues covered by advocates' immunity - that is, some complaints which relate to the way a lawyer handled a case in court, which cannot be complained about.

Who can complain?

Anyone affected by the way a complaint has been handled by the professional body - including private individuals and their representatives, groups of individuals, businesses, charities and other unincorporated bodies.

Representatives can bring a complaint on behalf of someone else, with the consent of the affected person.

Cost

Free to complainants.

Geographical limits

The practitioners concerned must come within the jurisdiction of the professional bodies for England and Wales.

There is no restriction on the complainant's place of residence.

Time limits

Complaints must be brought within 3 months of the date on which the professional body sent its written decision about the complaint to the complainant.

The Ombudsman has no power to waive this time limit.

Remedies

Financial compensation

Can be recommended against either the professional body or the practitioner concerned. It can include compensation for financial loss, distress or inconvenience. There is no formal maximum. For financial loss, the typical award is between £500 and £5,000 and the highest actual award in 1996 was £5,119. For distress, the typical award is between £250 and £500 and the highest award in 1996 was £1,750. For inconvenience, the typical award is between £100 and £200 and the highest award in 1996 was £350.

Can recommend the payment of interest on an award where the complainant has lost the opportunity to use a sum of money (for example, due to a delay by a solicitor in paying money held).

Can recommend the reimbursement of any reasonable expenses involved in referring the complaint to the Ombudsman.

The Ombudsman may take into account whether and to what extent the complainant caused his or her own problems.

Other

Can make a recommendation that the complaint is reconsidered by the professional body concerned or that the practitioner be disciplined by the professional body.

2. The complaints procedure

Making the complaint

Complainants must first have complained to the relevant professional body - but need not exhaust all its internal complaints procedures (see Exhausting the internal complaints procedure below).

Complaints must eventually be in writing (a guidance leaflet is available), but a phone call will start the process off, provided the complainant sends written confirmation within 3 months of the professional body's decision. The scheme prefers complainants to complete an application form, but this is not compulsory.

Exhausting the internal complaints procedure

Complainants can approach the Ombudsman directly, but must first have complained to the relevant professional body. Complainants are not required to exhaust all of the professional body's appeal procedures before approaching the Ombudsman, and the Ombudsman can intervene even where no decision has been made - for example, where he considers the professional body has unreasonably failed to start, or has delayed, its investigation.

Powers of investigation

Has the power to compel witnesses to attend to answer questions, and to produce documents.

Criteria for decisions

Places most emphasis on what is fair and reasonable.

Takes into account relevant codes of practice and good practice.

The Ombudsman is not strictly bound by earlier decisions, but does take them into account.

Confidentiality

Material supplied by the complainant is not routinely copied to the practitioner or professional body concerned. Documents can be submitted in confidence.

Individual reports are issued to the parties concerned, on a confidential basis. Noteworthy cases are published in the *Annual Report* and the scheme's newsletter. Complainants are not identified by name, practitioners are only identified by name if they have failed to comply with the Ombudsman's recommendation.

Stages in complaint resolution

Preliminary stage

The administrative support team scrutinises the application form and sends for the professional body's file. When the file arrives, a senior investigating officer reviews it and accepts the case if it meets the criteria for investigation.

If the complaint is not within the scheme's remit, the scheme secretary will notify the complainant and give reasons why the case cannot be accepted. Complainants may also be advised to approach another Ombudsman scheme or a citizens advice bureau or law centre.

Investigation

When a complaint is accepted for investigation, the complainant is notified and the case allocated to an investigating officer. He/she investigates and produces a draft report for the Ombudsman to consider. The Ombudsman's primary task is to review the professional body's handling of the complaint and there is usually sufficient information in the professional body's file and the complainant's letters/application form for that purpose. Where further information is needed, the Ombudsman may ask to examine the practitioner's file at first hand. The scheme provides for formal hearings (but none have so far been held).

Draft report

If the Ombudsman approves the draft report and it does not contain a recommendation directed at the practitioner or the professional body, it is finalised and signed by the Ombudsman. It goes to the complainant, the practitioner and the professional body.

If the draft report does contain a recommendation, it is seen first by the scheme's legal adviser before going to the Ombudsman. If the report recommends that the professional body should reconsider the case, the Ombudsman approves and signs the report and it is sent to the complainant, the scheme member and the professional body.

If the draft report recommends that the professional body, the practitioner or both should pay compensation, a preliminary view is prepared and, if approved by the Ombudsman, issued to the person or the professional body at whom the recommendation is directed, giving 28 days for a response. The professional body is also given the opportunity to respond to a preliminary view that the practitioner should pay compensation. The report is finalised by the legal adviser, taking any submissions into account. Where necessary, the complainant's view of any relevant new information will be obtained.

Final report

> This is approved by the Ombudsman and then issued. If a recommendation has been made, the parties at whom it is directed have 3 months to notify the Ombudsman of the steps they have taken, or that they are prepared to take, to comply.

Progress reports

> Complainants are informed in writing if an investigation is likely to take more than 6 months.

Types of ruling

Non-binding recommendation

> In 1996, 23% of complaints received resulted in an investigation followed by a recommendation against either the professional body or the practitioner concerned.

Formal criticism

> Of the way in which the complaint was dealt with by the professional body (8% of cases in 1996).

Formal decision

> That the complaint was dealt with adequately by the professional body concerned.

Rights of appeal against a decision

> There is no right of appeal against the Ombudsman's findings, but complainants who remain dissatisfied can still take the case to court.

> The scheme is subject to judicial review (no applications have so far reached a hearing).

Failure to comply with rulings

> Failure to comply must be publicised in whatever manner the Ombudsman specifies, at the scheme member's expense. (Members failed to comply in 2% of cases in the last 2 years: the publicity sanction was imposed in all cases.) When practitioners have not complied, it tends to be when they have been struck-off, declared

bankrupt, no longer in practice, or prepared to endure the publicity rather than comply. Professional bodies have so far always complied with recommendations.

How long does the process take?

Target timescale

Under review.

Actual timescale

Around 30% of complaints are dealt with within 6 months, 85% within 12 months.

Urgent cases (and cases of little obvious merit) are put on a fast-track procedure.

Delegation of decision-making

The Ombudsman has no deputy or equivalent. All reports are approved by the Ombudsman personally. The secretary to the scheme has a delegated power to refuse to investigate some complaints which the Ombudsman would otherwise be able to investigate (for instance, complaints involving internal legal professional matters which cause no detriment to clients).

If the Ombudsman faces a personal conflict of interest in any particular case, the Scottish Legal Services Ombudsman may be asked to deal with it instead.

Following up complaints

Complaints sent back to professional bodies are monitored. When a recommendation is addressed to a professional body or a practitioner, the Ombudsman asks for confirmation of compliance within 3 months of the date of the report. Failure to comply within that period is followed up. Post-report correspondence is monitored.

Complaining about the scheme itself

In the first instance, complaints are dealt with by the secretary to the scheme. Complainants who remain dissatisfied are referred to the Lord Chancellor's Department. (No statistics are kept: most complaints express dissatisfaction with the Ombudsman's decision rather than the way the case was handled.)

3. The scheme's structure and administration

Origins and membership

A statutory scheme, established under the Courts and Legal Services Act 1990. Started operating on 1 January 1991.

Structure and accountability

The Ombudsman is an independent public office-holder. He/she makes an Annual Report to the Lord Chancellor, which the Lord Chancellor lays before parliament.

The Ombudsman

Appointment

By the Lord Chancellor, who has the power of dismissal if the Ombudsman fails to maintain a high standard of conduct or to carry out his/her duties. The Ombudsman cannot be a legal practitioner.

Term of appointment

Up to 3 years, renewable.

Role

The Ombudsman oversees complaints handling in the legal profession.

Scheme's terms of reference

Laid down in the Courts and Legal Services Act 1990. Can only be changed by amending legislation or by general directions given by the Lord Chancellor.

Monitoring

Performance targets are published in the *Annual Report*.

BIOA member?

Yes.

Funding

Funded by the Lord Chancellor's Department.

Costs

Running cost

£648,000 in 1996/97 (excluding accommodation costs).

Cost per complaint

Not published.

Staffing

Overall responsibility

The Ombudsman.

Staff

A secretary and a legal adviser. 14 investigative staff who are usually experienced case-workers, not necessarily legally qualified but with some knowledge of the legal system/profession (of whom 6 work part-time from home), 6 administrative staff.

Forthcoming changes

Changes in the professional bodies, such as the relaunch of the Solicitors Complaints Bureau as the Office for the Supervision of Solicitors in September 1996 and the Bar Council's introduction of a new complaints system in 1997, will not affect the Ombudsman's role.

Michael Barnes retires as Ombudsman in September and a new Ombudsman will take up office on 22 September 1997.

Improving best practice

By law, the Ombudsman is entitled to make recommendations to the professional bodies about their general arrangements for dealing with complaints, and to refer relevant matters to the Lord Chancellor's advisory committee on legal education and conduct. The Ombudsman holds regular liaison meetings with the professional bodies.

Facts and figures

Numbers of new complaints received in writing

Subject of complaint	1995	1996	% change
Divorce/family proceedings	324	383	18.0
House sale/purchase	260	273	5.0
Miscellaneous civil litigation (new category)	179	256	43.0
Administration of wills	169	221	31.0
Personal injury	157	161	2.5
Landlord/tenant	97	121	25.0
Criminal proceedings	94	153	63.0
Property disputes	88	119	35.0
Employment/contractual disputes	62	70	13.0
Professional negligence claims	22	43	95.0
Other	452	473	5.0

Numbers of complaints at each stage of procedure

	1995	1996	% change
Total complaints handled	2,910	3,097	6.0
Complaints sent back to internal procedures	271	225	-17.0
Not within remit/referred elsewhere			
Complaints not pursued for other reasons	582	443	-24.0
Complaints awaiting file from professional body and other processing	153	156	2.0
Investigations pending at end of year	863	885	2.5
Reports issued	1,041	1,388	33.0

Outcome of complaints fully investigated

Complaints upheld	190 (18%)	321 (23%)	-
Complaint upheld in part	70 (7%)	90 (8%)	-
Complaint not upheld	781 (75%)	989 (71%)	-

Information available about the scheme

Publicising the scheme

The three professional bodies must inform complainants about their right to refer their case to the Legal Services Ombudsman.

The scheme is publicised through the *Annual Report* and through press articles and legal programmes on TV and radio.

A newsletter goes to citizens advice bureaux, other advice centres, law centres and the profession.

Also publishes a guidance leaflet to using the scheme and regular yearly bulletins.

Terms of reference

Published in the *Annual Report*.

Annual Report

Published in June. In addition to tables above, includes further detail on casework flows, analyses of complaints against the various professional groupings and by size of firm, analyses of investigations by type of legal transaction and by reason for complaint.

Other publications

R. James and M. Seneviratne, 'The Legal Services Ombudsman - Form versus Function?', *Modern Law Review*, March 1995.

Scottish Legal Services Ombudsman

2 Greenside Lane, Edinburgh EH1 3AH
Tel: 0131 556 5574. Fax: 0131 556 1519

Ombudsman: Garry S. Watson

1. Using the scheme: key points

Service-providers covered

The Law Society of Scotland (solicitors).

Faculty of Advocates (advocates).

The Scottish Conveyancing and Executry Services Board (conveyancing and executry practitioners).

Complaints covered

Any complaint about the way in which the professional bodies listed above have handled a complaint about professional misconduct by one of their members or inadequate professional services or the unwillingness of a professional body to investigate a complaint.

Includes complaints that are already subject to court proceedings or on which a court has already ruled (but see Complaints not covered below).

Complaints not covered

Cannot investigate the original complaint, only how the complaint was handled by the practitioner's professional body.

The Law Society of Scotland will not investigate a complaint against one of its members (or will suspend an ongoing investigation) if legal action is taken. The Ombudsman cannot become involved until the Law Society has completed its investigation.

Who can complain?

Individuals, businesses, partnerships, charities and other unincorporated bodies.

Friends, relatives or legal representatives can complain on behalf of someone living.

Complaints are not usually accepted from the representatives of a dead person.

Cost

Free to complainants.

Geographical limits

There is no restriction on the complainant's place of residence.

The legal practitioners concerned must come within the jurisdiction of the professional bodies for Scotland.

Time limits

Complaints must be lodged within 6 months of the date on which the professional body sent its written decision about the complaint to the complainant. The Ombudsman has no discretion to waive this time limit.

Remedies

Financial compensation

The Ombudsman can make any recommendation to the professional body which is considered appropriate, including a recommendation that the professional body should pay financial compensation.

Other

Can forward a complaint about the professional conduct of a solicitor or the inadequacy of professional services provided to the Scottish Solicitors Discipline Tribunal.

2. The complaints procedure

Making the complaint

Complaints must be in writing. There is a guidance leaflet. There is no standard complaint form. Where the complainant has difficulty presenting a complaint, the Ombudsman may invite the complainant to a meeting or recommend that he or she seeks help from a citizens advice bureau.

Exhausting the internal complaints procedure

Before the Ombudsman can investigate, the professional body's complaints-handling system must first be exhausted. Complainants are then advised by the professional body that they may refer the complaint to the Ombudsman if they are dissatisfied with how it has been handled.

Powers of investigation

The Ombudsman has no direct powers of investigation, but may request the professional body concerned to provide any information that may reasonably be required. Cannot require individuals to attend hearings.

If the Ombudsman faces a personal conflict of interest in any particular case, the Legal Services Ombudsman for England and Wales may be asked to deal with it instead.

Criteria for decisions

Most emphasis is placed on what is fair and reasonable and on impartiality.

Takes account of relevant codes of practice.

Takes account of previous decisions, but each investigation is determined on its merits.

Confidentiality

Summaries of cases illustrating the scheme's work are included in the *Annual Report*: the complainant and the professional practitioner concerned are not identified by name; the professional body is named.

Stages in complaint resolution

Preliminary stage

When a complaint is received, enquiries may have to be made with the complainant to establish whether the complaint is eligible.

If a complaint is not within the scheme's remit, the complainant is told where the complaint should be directed, if known (complaints are not forwarded automatically).

Investigation

Assuming the complaint is eligible, the scheme's complaints investigator calls for the professional body's file which contains its correspondence with the complainant and with the practitioner complained against. The complaints investigator reviews the file and prepares a draft opinion, which includes the background to the case, comments and a conclusion. If matters need to be clarified with the complainant or with the professional body, it will be done at this stage. The Ombudsman then reviews the draft opinion and the complainant may be invited to attend a meeting at the Ombudsman's office - but only where it is necessary to clarify the nature of the complaint or the facts surrounding it.

Final opinion

The Ombudsman finalises the opinion. The final opinion goes to the complainant, with copies to the professional body and the practitioner concerned.

Progress reports

Not usually sent to the complainant, unless the time taken to investigate is longer than originally indicated. Complaints are dealt with in strictly chronological order.

Types of ruling

Formal opinion

This is not binding on the professional body.

Rights of appeal against a decision

There is no right of appeal against the Ombudsman's formal opinions.

There is no specific provision that the scheme is subject to judicial review.

Failure to comply with recommendations

The Ombudsman has no powers to enforce recommendations. In 1995 and 1996, the Law Society of Scotland declined to take action in response to the Ombudsman's recommendations in 13% and 17% of cases respectively. In 1995 the Faculty of Advocates rejected the Ombudsman's recommendations on the one critical opinion issued relating to it; in 1996 it accepted, in part, the recommendations on the one critical opinion issued.

Has the power to publish the refusal of a professional body to comply with recommendations.

How long does the process take?

From receiving the professional body's file to the issue of an opinion: usually between 2 and 4 months.

Delegation of decision-making

There is no Deputy Ombudsman. The Ombudsman's powers are not delegated in any way.

Following up complaints

If a complaint has not yet exhausted the professional body's complaints-handling system, its progress may be reviewed.

To monitor whether a decision by the Ombudsman has been complied with, a file is brought up at regular intervals until the case is closed.

Complaining about the scheme itself

There is no fixed procedure. The Ombudsman deals personally with complaints about the handling of a case. (No statistics are kept, although some complaints about the scheme are from complainants whose complaints have not been upheld and are critical of the Ombudsman's opinion.)

3. The scheme's structure and administration

Origins and membership

A statutory scheme, established under the Law Reform (Miscellaneous Provisions) (Scotland) Act 1990. Started operating on 3 June 1991.

Structure and accountability

The Ombudsman is an independent public office holder. He makes an *Annual Report* to the Secretary of State for Scotland which is laid before Parliament.

The Ombudsman

Appointment

By the Secretary of State for Scotland, who may terminate the appointment if he/she believes termination to be desirable. The Ombudsman may not be a practising solicitor or advocate.

Term of appointment

3 years, renewable at the Secretary of State's discretion.

Role

Overall responsibility for running the office and complaints-handling.

Scheme's terms of reference

These are laid down in the Law Reform (Miscellaneous Provisions) (Scotland) Act 1990.

Can only be changed by amending legislation or through general directions issued by the Secretary of State for Scotland.

Monitoring

A statement of operating principles appeared in the 1996 *Annual Report.*

BIOA member?

Yes.

Funding

Funding comes from the Scottish Office.

Costs

Not published.

Staffing

Overall responsibility

The Ombudsman.

Staff

2 - a complaints investigator (who has a law degree but has never worked as a solicitor) and an office secretary - both work 4 days a week. The Ombudsman also has a legal adviser within the Scottish Office.

Forthcoming changes

None.

Improving best practice

The Ombudsman can make recommendations to a professional body relating to the way in which it handles complaints, and to the Secretary of State for Scotland relating to the Ombudsman's remit. He has regular meetings with the bodies covered by the scheme. He takes part in the Law Society's yearly professional responsibility roadshows around university law schools.

Facts and figures

Numbers of complaint completed

Subject of complaint	1995	1996	% change
Civil action (non-matrimonial)	42	51	21.0
Conveyancing	41	28	-31.0
Civil action (matrimonial)	10	12	[1]
Executry of deceased persons' estates	9	10	[1]
Criminal action	5	6	[1]
Other	7	1	[1]

[1] Numbers too small for percentages to be significant.

Numbers of complaints at each stage of procedure

	1995	1996	% change
Total complaints handled	323	315	-2.5
Complaints not within remit/referred elsewhere	136	132	-2.9
Complaints not pursued for other reasons	38	15	-60.5
Other complaints (including investigations in progress)	33	60	81.8
Opinions issued	113[1]	108[1]	-4.4

Outcome of complaints fully investigated

Complaint upheld	39 (35%)	55 (51%)	-
Complaint not upheld	74 (65%)	53 (49%)	-

[1] Excluding cases dealt with on behalf of the Legal Services Ombudsman for England and Wales (3 in 1995, none in 1996).

Information available about the scheme

Publicising the scheme

Publicity about the scheme is mainly through the *Annual Report* and the press conference at which it is launched. A leaflet about the scheme is available from the Ombudsman.

Terms of reference

Published in the *Annual Report*.

Annual Report

Usually published in April. In addition to the tables above, it includes further information on caseflows, reasons for complaints being ineligible, nature of complaints, nature of criticisms made against the professional bodies, and how the complaints were handled by the professional bodies.

Local Government Ombudsman for England

(The Commission for Local Administration in England)

For Greater London, Kent and East Sussex:

21 Queen Anne's Gate, London SW1H 9BU
Tel: 0171 915 3210. Fax: 0171 233 0396
Ombudsman: Edward Osmotherly CB

For East Anglia, the South-West, West, South and most of central England (except Birmingham):

The Oaks No. 2, Westwood Way, Westwood Business Park,
Coventry CV4 8JB
Tel: 01203 695999. Fax: 01203 695902
Ombudsman: Jerry White

For Cheshire, Derbyshire, Nottinghamshire, Lincolnshire, Birmingham and the North of England:

Beverley House, 17 Shipton Road, York YO3 6FZ
Tel: 01904 663200. Fax: 01904 663269
Ombudsman: Patricia Thomas

1. Using the scheme: key points

Service-providers covered

The following authorities in England:

- district, borough, city and county councils (not town or parish councils) and their joint boards and committees;

- the Commission for New Towns (housing complaints only);

- urban development corporations and English Partnerships (town and country planning complaints only);

- housing action trusts;

- police authorities (not individual police officers) and fire authorities;

- National Park authorities, the Norfolk and Suffolk Broads Authority and (for flood defence and land drainage complaints only) the Environment Agency ;

- education appeal committees.

Complaints covered

Complaints that personal injustice has been caused by an authority's maladministration (administrative failures).

Complaints not covered

Actions affecting all - or most - of the inhabitants of the area of the authority in question.

Cases where the complainant has a right of appeal to a tribunal, government minister or court (although the Ombudsman can decide to investigate if he/she is satisfied that using the alternative is not reasonable).

Complaints about the commencement or conduct of court proceedings.

Complaints about policy decisions or the exercise of an authority's discretion where there is no maladministration.

Complaints about action taken in connection with the investigation or prevention of crime.

Complaints about teaching, internal management or discipline within schools and colleges.

Complaints about commercial or contractual matters (except for land transactions).

Personnel matters.

Who can complain?

Individuals, groups of people, businesses, partnerships, charities and unincorporated bodies.

Relatives, friends and legal representatives on another person's behalf, provided they have proper authorisation; relatives, beneficiaries and legal representatives on behalf of a dead person.

A local councillor can act on behalf of a complainant, provided the complainant consents. But one local authority cannot complain about another local authority and individual local councillors cannot complain about the actions of their own authority in their capacity as members.

Cost

Free to complainants.

Geographical limits

Complaints must be against the authorities in England listed above (see Service-providers covered).

There is no restriction on the complainant's place of residence.

Time limits

Complaints must usually be made within 12 months of the day on which the complainant was first aware of the problem.

The Ombudsman can investigate a complaint made after the 12-month limit if he/she considers it reasonable to do so.

Remedies

Financial compensation

There is no maximum limit on the amount the Ombudsman can recommend. May include compensation for actual loss, loss of a non-monetary benefit, loss of actual value, lost opportunity, distress, time and trouble.

May recommend interest be paid on compensation (for example, where money owed to the complainant was not paid at the proper time).

May reduce the amount of compensation to take account of the complainant's conduct, for example where delays were partly the complainant's fault.

Other

The Ombudsman can recommend any practical action that would be a suitable remedy for the injustice to the complainant or that an authority change its policies and procedures.

2. The complaints procedure

Making the complaint

Complainants can approach the Ombudsman direct or through an intermediary such as a local councillor.

Complaints must be in writing. The scheme's guidance leaflet includes a standard complaint form (although this is not obligatory). There is a centralised telephone advice service. Staff will help people with writing difficulties by filling in a form over the telephone and sending it to them for signature. Complaints in languages other than English are accepted.

Exhausting the internal complaints procedure

The authority must have had a reasonable opportunity to investigate and reply to the complaint. The Ombudsman usually asks the complainant for evidence of a written complaint made to a senior officer or member of the authority - and, if the complainant has received one, the authority's response. When a complaint reaches the scheme too soon, it is sent on to the chief executive of the authority concerned: if the authority has not investigated and replied within 3 months, the Ombudsman will usually accept the complaint for investigation.

Powers of investigation

The same powers as the High Court to call and examine witnesses, and to require the production of documents. People who try to obstruct an investigation can be found in contempt of court.

Criteria for decisions

Whether there has been maladministration in the way a decision was reached, taking into account the law, good practice and what is fair and reasonable.

Aims to be consistent with previous rulings.

Confidentiality

Investigation reports are publicised - the complainant is not named, the authority is. These reports go to the local media in the area of the authority concerned, unless the Ombudsman decides against this (for example, to avoid risk of violence to a complainant) and sometimes the national media. The authority concerned has to make the report available for public inspection for 3 weeks.

Stages in complaint resolution

Initial scrutiny

One of the investigating staff screens each complaint. If the authority concerned has not yet had a reasonable chance to deal with it (called a premature complaint), a copy is sent to the authority concerned and the complainant is asked to re-submit the complaint to the Ombudsman if he/she remains dissatisfied.

If the complaint is not within the Ombudsman's jurisdiction (or there is no evidence of injustice or fault), the complainant is usually told within 28 days and, where relevant, redirected to the person or body to whom the complaint should be made.

Investigation

Eligible complaints are allocated to an investigating officer, who will ask the authority concerned for its comments. The officer may also examine the authority's files, visit the complainant or visit any site involved. The officer tries to achieve a settlement wherever possible: failing that, the complaint is either rejected (if there is no evidence of fault or injustice or if, on further investigation, it proves to be outside the Ombudsman's jurisdiction) or is investigated further.

If a complaint is rejected at this stage, the complainant can make a case for further consideration.

The decision to investigate a complaint further is usually taken by an assistant director, on the recommendation of the investigating officer. The case may now be allocated to a different investigating officer. At this stage, it is usually necessary to inspect the authority's files and to interview the complainant and/or his or her representatives (occasionally together), as well as any authority staff or members involved. If the case is settled or it becomes clear during the investigation that there has been no maladministration and/or injustice, a discontinuation letter is sent to the complainant. If a matter of public interest is involved, a discontinuation report may be drafted for publication.

Draft factual report

This is issued after the investigation. It sets out the facts of the case (leaving out the conclusions) and goes to the complainant, the authority and any other interested party for their comments. At the same time the authority is told about any criticisms the Ombudsman is likely to make and invited to comment on them.

Final report

This includes any recommendations to the authority and is decided by the Ombudsman. The report is issued to the complainant, the authority and usually the press.

Further report

If an authority does not respond satisfactorily to the formal report's recommendations within 3 months (or longer, with the Ombudsman's agreement) or if it does not take the recommended action within another 3 months, the Ombudsman issues a further report - setting out those facts and making recommendations. If this is not complied with, the Ombudsman can instruct the authority to publish a statement in the local press, giving details of what was recommended in the further report; the authority may include its reasons for non-compliance.

Progress reports

> Complainants are informed of progress at least every 6 weeks and always receive a letter at key stages during the investigation.

Types of ruling

Local settlement

> Where the authority agrees to provide a remedy satisfactory to the Ombudsman without the need for a formal report. (In 1995/96 around 22% of cases were settled in this way.)

Formal report

> Recommendations in a formal report are not legally binding.

Rights of appeal against a decision

> If there has been a decision without a formal investigation, the complainant can ask the Ombudsman to reconsider the complaint if, for example, there is some new evidence.

> There is no right of appeal to an outside body. Judicial review may be sought in the High Court (there have been 5 judicial reviews in the scheme's lifetime).

> The Ombudsman cannot refer points of law to the courts.

Failure to comply with rulings

Failure to comply with a recommendation

> The Ombudsman can issue a further report.

Failure to comply with a further report

> The Ombudsman can require the authority to publish a statement in the local press.

> (Research has shown that the most common reasons for non-compliance are that the authority did not agree maladministration had occurred or, where it accepted there had been maladministration, considered that this had not caused injustice to the complainant.)

How long does the process take?

Target timescale

For 1996/97 premature complaints - 3 weeks. For other complaints, to complete settlement stage - 11 weeks; to complete formal investigation 46 - weeks.

Delegation of decision-making

The Ombudsman personally decides complaints which are the subject of formal reports, plus novel or very contentious cases.

In the Ombudsman's absence, the Deputy Ombudsmen can act for him or her (except in the most contentious cases), including signing formal reports. The Ombudsman personally monitors 10% of cases terminated by investigating staff. Deputy Ombudsmen and investigating staff take most decisions involving complaints outside the Ombudsman's jurisdiction or where there appears to be no maladministration or injustice.

Following up complaints

The authority must tell the Ombudsman when recommendations have been complied with. Until then, the scheme maintains contact with the complainant.

Complaining about the scheme itself

There is a formal written procedure. (113 complaints were received in 1995/96, of which 34 were partly or fully upheld.)

3. The scheme's structure and administration

Origins and membership

A statutory scheme set up by the Local Government Act 1974 and, by law, covering all the authorities listed above (see Service-providers covered). Started operating in 1975.

Structure and accountability

Membership

Consists of the 3 Local Commissioners (or Local Government Ombudsmen) and the Parliamentary Commissioner (Parliamentary Ombudsman) ex officio.

Role

To give general advice and guidance to authorities: to review the operation of the scheme every 3 years; to publish a combined *Annual Report*, accounts and other information; to provide central services, such as offices; and to ensure the efficient and effective use of resources. As a body the Commission has no power to review an Ombudsman's decision.

The three Ombudsmen

Appointment

By the Queen, on the recommendation of the Secretary of State for the Environment, after consulting representatives of local authorities. (Posts are advertised and a selection committee makes a recommendation.) Can be removed from office on grounds of incapacity or misbehaviour. Term of appointment: no maximum, but must retire at 65.

Role

Responsible for the examination of complaints in his/her geographical area.

Scheme's terms of reference

Set out in the Local Government Act 1974 and summarised in the Commission's *Annual Report* and leaflet. Can only be changed by amending legislation. Every 3 years, the Commission reviews the operation of the legislation and makes necessary recommendations to government departments.

Monitoring

Values and objectives are published in the *Annual Report*, and business goals in the business plan. Some targets, like timescales, are published in leaflets.

The Commission monitors complainants' ethnic origins and any disabilities through an equal opportunities form.

In 1995 the Commission used a customer satisfaction survey to help formulate its key objectives.

Investigating staff get detailed internal procedure notes and cases are discussed at regular meetings.

BIOA member?

Yes.

Funding

Through the Department of the Environment, yearly.

Costs

Running cost

£7,343,470 in 1995/96.

Cost per complaint

£449 in 1995/96.

Staffing

Overall responsibility

The three Ombudsmen are responsible for their own offices.

Casework staff

> 3 Deputy Ombudsmen (each accountable to an Ombudsman), 12 assistant directors, 96 investigating staff (all graduates or equivalent, not necessarily in law or local government).

Administration staff

> 75, plus a central administration group of 20 headed by the secretary to the Commission.

Forthcoming changes

> A fundamental review of the Commission was completed in August 1996. The Secretary of State for the Environment subsequently announced the service would continue. The review's recommendations addressed to the Commission are now being implemented.

Improving best practice

> The Commission gives advice and guidance to authorities on good administrative practice (in guidance notes on good practice and bulletins). It also aims to improve standards through: comments and recommendations in published investigation reports; contributions to conferences and seminars; advice and assistance to bodies which advise local authorities and to local authorities themselves, on request.

Facts and figures

Number of complaints received

Subject of complaint	1994/95	1995/96	% change
Housing	5,801	5,726	-1.2
Planning	3,546	3,370	-5.0
Community charge, rating	1,334	1,141	-14.5
Education	1,187	1,112	-6.3
Highways	999	1,056	5.7
Social services	838	936	11.7
Environmental health	536	630	17.5
Land	284	301	6.0
Leisure and recreation	142	178	25.4
Drainage	254	128	-49.6
Commercial	100	131	31.0
Personnel	111	121	9.0
Consumer protection	57	68	19.3
Transport	10	20	100.0
Water	21	16	-23.8
Fire	7	6	[1]
Police	5	4	[1]
Miscellaneous	293	322	9.9
Total	15,525	15,266	-1.7

[1] Numbers too small for percentages to be significant.

Numbers of complaints at each stage of procedure

	1994/95	1995/96	% change
Total complaints determined	15,140	16,344	8.0
Complaints sent back to internal procedures (premature complaints)	2,166	2,759	27.4
Complaints outside jurisdiction	1,771	2,013	13.7
Complaints not pursued because no maladministration or no or insufficient injustice	8,045	8,483	5.4
Complaints for which formal public report was issued	602	536	-10.9
Remedy provided without need for formal report ('local settlement')	2,556	2,552	-0.2

Outcome of complaints fully investigated

Complaint where maladministration and injustice found	518 (86%)	410 (76.5%)	-
Complaint where maladministration but not injustice found	60 (10%)	76 (14%)	-
Complaint where no maladministration	24 (4%)	50 (9.5%)	-

Information available about the scheme

Publicising the scheme

Leaflets and posters about the scheme are sent to libraries, citizens advice bureaux and other advice agencies, MPs (for England) and local authorities.

Terms of reference

Summarised in the scheme's *Annual Report* and leaflet.

Annual Report

Published in September. Includes figures on complaints received and determined; complaints determined per member of staff; detailed breakdowns of time taken to deal with complaints; staff numbers; financial accounts for the year; reasons why complaints were 'terminated'; lists of reports by authority; and causes of maladministration.

Other publications

Commission for Local Administration in England, *Remedies: Non-Compliance*, 1996.

E.B.C. Osmotherly (editor), *Guide to the Local Government Ombudsman Service*, Pitman Publishing, 1995.

Commission for Local Administration in England, *Disposal of Land: Guidance on Good Practice 5*, 1995.

Commission for Local Administration in England, *Members' Interest: Guidance on Good Practice 4*, 1994.

Commission for Local Administration in England, *Council Housing Repairs: Guidance on Good Practice 3*, 1993.

Commission for Local Administration in England, *Good Administrative Practice: Guidance on Good Practice 2*, 1993.

Commission for Local Administration in England, *Devising a Complaints System: Guidance on Good Practice 1*, 1992.

Commission for Local Administration in England, *Local Government Ombudsman Bulletin*, issues 1 (July 1993) to 7 (December 1996).

Also publishes and publicises an annual business plan, regular bulletins and guidance notes for authorities, and formal investigation reports and a digest of significant cases.

Local Government Ombudsman for Scotland

(The Commissioner for Local Administration in Scotland)

23 Walker Street, Edinburgh EH3 7HX
Tel: 0131 225 5300. Fax: 0131 225 9495

Ombudsman: Frederick C. Marks

1. Using the scheme: key points

Service-providers covered

The following authorities in Scotland:

- local authorities and their joint boards and committees;

- licensing boards;

- Scottish Homes (as landlord);

- Strathclyde Passenger Transport Authority.

Complaints covered

Complaints that injustice has been caused by maladministration (or administrative failures).

Complaints not covered

Action affecting all - or most - of the inhabitants of the area of the authority in question.

Cases where the complainant has the right of appeal to a tribunal, government minister or court (although the Ombudsman can decide to investigate if he is satisfied that using the alternative remedy is not reasonable).

Complaints concerning the commencement or handling of court proceedings.

Complaints about policy decisions, the exercise of discretion not involving maladministration, and personnel matters.

Complaints about action taken in connection with the investigation or prevention of crime.

Complaints about teaching, internal management or discipline within schools and colleges.

Complaints about commercial or contractual matters (except for land transactions).

Complaints on which a court has already ruled, or which are already subject to court proceedings. Where court action is contemplated, the Ombudsman has discretion over whether or not to investigate.

Who can complain?

Individuals, groups of people, businesses, partnerships, charities and unincorporated bodies.

Relatives, friends and legal representatives can complain on another person's behalf so long as they are properly authorised.

Relatives, beneficiaries and legal representatives can complain on behalf of a dead person.

A local councillor can act on behalf of a complainant, provided the complainant consents. But one local authority cannot complain against another local authority and individual local councillors cannot complain about the decisions of their own authority in their capacity as members.

Cost

Free to complainants.

Geographical limits

Complaints must be against the authorities in Scotland listed above (see Service-providers covered).

There is no restriction on the complainant's place of residence.

Time limits

Complaints must usually be made within 12 months of the day on which the complainant was first aware of the problem.

The Ombudsman can investigate a complaint made after the 12-month limit if he considers it reasonable to do so.

Remedies

Financial compensation

No maximum on the amount the Ombudsman can recommend.

Can include interest on compensation in cases of undue delay.

May occasionally recommend that the authority concerned pays the complainant's legal or other expert costs where these were incurred because of the authority's fault.

May occasionally reduce the amount of compensation if the actions of complainants or those acting on their behalf contributed to the problem.

Other

The Ombudsman can recommend corrective action, such as restoring complainants to their previous position, carrying out specific actions, or reviewing procedures and cases.

2. The complaints procedure

Making the complaint

Complainants can approach the scheme direct or through an intermediary such as a local councillor. Complaints must be in writing. A standard complaints form is available but not obligatory.

Exhausting the internal complaints procedure

Complainants must complain in writing to the authority concerned before complaining to the Ombudsman and give reasonable time for a response. If the authority does not respond in a reasonable time, the complaint can be taken up by the Ombudsman.

Powers of investigation

Power to call and examine witnesses and to require documents to be produced. People who try to obstruct investigations can be held in contempt.

Criteria for decisions

What is fair and reasonable in the circumstances, taking into account the law, codes of practice and recognised good or best practice.

The Ombudsman seeks consistency with previous decisions, but is not bound by them.

Confidentiality

Formal reports are usually published by the authority concerned, and academics, researchers, pressure groups and the press request copies of some or all. Complainants are not named; the name of the authority concerned is included. The Ombudsman may occasionally order that a case report is not published, usually to protect the complainant.

All case reports are summarised in the *Annual Report*.

Stages in complaint resolution

Screening

Incoming mail is screened to see whether it is within the scheme's jurisdiction.

If a complaint is not within jurisdiction, where possible, the complainant is re-directed to another complaints-handling body.

Assessment

Complaints which appear to be within jurisdiction are allocated to an investigating officer who seeks any necessary clarification from the complainant, possibly in a visit. The officer may also have informal contact with the authority. If the case is settled or a decision is taken not to proceed to a formal investigation (because maladministration and injustice do not appear to have taken place, for instance), both parties to the complaint are informed and the file is closed.

Enquiry

In cases which go on to this stage, the authority concerned is asked for relevant information and any comments. The investigating officer may also try to facilitate a settlement. Cases not determined at this stage become subject to formal investigation.

Formal investigation

The file may now be allocated to a different investigating officer. He/she examines the documents and interviews the complainant, local councillors and staff as necessary (hearings involving both parties are not held). The case may be settled at this stage, if so the Ombudsman will issue a short report giving his reasons for discontinuing the investigation.

Report stage

If the case has not been settled, the investigating officer will produce a draft report. Following approval by the Ombudsman or the Deputy Ombudsman, this is issued to the authority, the complainant and any interested parties for comment. After taking comments into account and obtaining any further information necessary, the investigating officer prepares a draft of the final report. When this has been approved and signed by the Ombudsman, it is issued to both parties and to the press. If the Ombudsman is not satisfied with the authority's response to his final report, he will issue a further report.

Progress reports

Complainants are informed of the progress of their case by monthly letter or as each stage in the procedure is reached.

Types of ruling

Informal conciliation

> 21.4% of all complaints received and 33.3% of all complaints taken up were settled in this way in 1996/97.

Formal report

> Issued in 2.1% of cases in 1996/97.

> The majority of cases - 74.5% in 1996/97 - are not formally investigated either because the complaint is not within the scheme's remit or there is no evidence of injustice and maladministration.

Rights of appeal against a decision

> After receiving the letter explaining that it has been decided not to conduct a formal investigation, the complainant normally has 14 days within which to make any comments and ask the Ombudsman to reconsider the decision (about 10% of complainants do so).

> There is no right of appeal against a decision in a formal report.

> It is not established whether the scheme is subject to judicial review.

> The Ombudsman cannot refer particular points of law to the courts.

> Failure to comply with rulings

Failure to comply with a recommendation

> This happens in about 6% of cases. The Ombudsman will issue a further report (24 have been issued in the scheme's lifetime).

Failure to comply with the recommendation of a further report

> The Ombudsman can require the authority to make a public statement in a newspaper of its reasons for non-compliance and give the Ombudsman an opportunity to reply (a sanction so far imposed twice).

How long does the process take?

Target timescale

6 weeks for assessment decisions, 6 months for formal reports.

Actual timescale

Just under 4 and a half months (19 weeks) for formal reports in 1996/97.

Delegation of decision-making

The Deputy Ombudsman (who is also the scheme's secretary) acts as chief executive and can deputise for the Ombudsman in all respects. The Deputy Ombudsman makes day-to-day decisions on investigation and non-investigation of cases, and all decision letters are signed by her or in her name. The Ombudsman approves and usually signs all formal reports.

Following up complaints

Complaints not within the scheme's remit or which are not investigated are not followed up.

Where a formal report is issued, the authority concerned is required by law to let the Ombudsman know within 3 months of its issue whether or not it has complied with its recommendations.

Complaining about the scheme itself

Complaints are investigated by the Deputy Ombudsman: if the complainant remains dissatisfied, he or she can ask the Ombudsman to consider the complaint. The procedure is set out in the scheme's charter standard statement.

3. The scheme's structure and administration

Origins and membership

A statutory scheme set up by the Local Government (Scotland) Act 1975 (as subsequently amended) and, by law, covering all the authorities listed above (see Service-providers covered). Started operating in 1976.

Structure and accountability

There is no body responsible for overseeing the work of the scheme. It is financially accountable to the Accounts Commission for Scotland.

The Ombudsman

Appointment

By the Crown, on the recommendation of the Secretary of State for Scotland. Can be removed on the grounds of incapacity or misbehaviour.

Term of appointment

No maximum, but must retire at 65. (It is a part-time appointment.)

Role

To oversee the examination and investigation of complaints.

Scheme's terms of reference

Laid down by the Local Government (Scotland) Act 1975. Can only be changed by amending legislation (although the restrictions on jurisdiction can be lifted by statutory instrument).

Monitoring

Research into the scheme's effectiveness has been published by independent researchers (see Other publications below).

BIOA member?

Yes.

Funding

By a levy on local authorities by the Accounts Commission for Scotland, based on the population of the 32 local authorities covered by the scheme.

Costs

Running cost

£551,000 in 1996/97 (includes special provision for renewal of computer system). (£432,000 in 1995/96.)

Cost per complaint

Not published.

Staffing

Overall responsibility

The secretary (who is also the Deputy Ombudsman).

Staff

6 investigating staff (most have experience of working in the public sector) and 4 administrative staff.

Forthcoming changes

The scheme was reviewed in 1995/96. Following the 1995 review of local government in Scotland, the government also announced its intention to extend the scheme's jurisdiction to include complaints against individual councillors in Scotland. A Bill to do this was given Royal Assent in March 1997.

Improving best practice

The Ombudsman can issue best practice guidelines. In general he uses individual and annual reports to highlight issues relating to good practice.

Facts and figures

New complaints received in writing (including ineligible complaints)

Subject of complaint	1995/96	1996/97	% change
Housing	394	296	-24.8
Planning	179	161	-10.1
Land and property	92	77	-16.3
Council tax/rates	54	69	27.8
Social work	29	41	41.4
Water and sewerage	26	-[1]	-
Roads	25	32	28.0
Environmental health	22	14	-36.4
Building control	20	19	-5.0
Education	19	25	31.6
Other complaints within jurisdiction	85	70	-17.6
Other complaints outside jurisdiction	83	69	-16.9

[1] Now out of scope following creation of water authorities in Scotland.

Numbers of complaints at each stage of procedure

	1995/96	1996/97	% change
Total complaints handled	1,065	891	-16.3
Complaints not within remit/referred elsewhere	83	69	-16.9
Complaints not pursued for other reasons	358	300	-16.2
Complaints reaching enquiry stage	521	493	-5.4
Complaints reaching formal investigation	17	19	-[1]

Outcome of complaints fully investigated

Complaint upheld	11	8
Complaint upheld in part	4	-
Complaint not upheld	1	-
Complaints discontinued as settled	4	6

[1] Too small for percentages to be significant.

Information available about the scheme

Publicising the scheme

Local authorities usually mention the existence of the scheme in their own internal complaints procedures. Leaflets about the scheme are issued to local authorities (for display in libraries and public offices) and to citizens advice bureaux.

Terms of reference

Described in the scheme leaflet.

Annual Report

Published in July or August. In addition to the tables above it includes analyses of complaints not accepted for formal investigation and a list of individual case reports.

Other publications

Janice H. Renton, *Twenty Years On - the Local Government Ombudsman reviewed*, Commissioner for Local Administration in Scotland, 1996.

Katherine Thompson, *The Office of the Commissioner for Local Administration in Scotland - a socio-legal study of its nature and effectiveness*, unpublished PhD dissertation, Glasgow Polytechnic, July 1991.

James G. Logie and Paul Q. Waterman, *The Local Ombudsman*, T & T Clark (Edinburgh), 1990.

The Ombudsman also publishes a Charter Standard Statement and a good practice note on setting up a complaints system.

Local Government Ombudsman for Wales

(The Commission for Local Administration in Wales)

Derwen House, Court Road, Bridgend CF31 1BN
Tel: 01656 661 325. Fax: 01656 658317

Commissioner (Ombudsman): Elwyn R. Moseley

1. Using the scheme: key points

Service-providers covered

The following authorities in Wales:

- local authorities, and their joint boards and committees (but not town or community councils);

- the Land Authority for Wales;

- the Development Board for Rural Wales (in connection with its housing functions before April 1996);

- police authorities (not individual police officers) and fire authorities;

- National Park authorities and the flood defence functions of the Environment Agency.

Complaints covered

Complaints that personal injustice has been caused by an authority's maladministration (or administrative failures).

Complaints not covered

A problem affecting all, or most of, the inhabitants of the area of the authority in question.

Cases where the complainant has the right of appeal to a tribunal, government minister or court (although the Ombudsman can decide to investigate if he is satisfied that using the alternative remedy is not reasonable).

Complaints concerning the bringing or handling of court proceedings.

Complaints about policy decisions, the exercise of discretion not involving maladministration, or personnel matters.

Complaints about action taken in connection with the investigation or prevention of crime.

Complaints about teaching, internal management or discipline within schools and colleges.

Complaints about commercial or contractual matters (except for land transactions).

Complaints on which a court has already ruled or which are already subject to court proceedings. Where court action is contemplated, the Ombudsman has discretion over whether or not to investigate.

Who can complain?

Individuals, groups of people, businesses, partnerships, charities and unincorporated bodies.

Relatives, friends and legal representatives on another person's behalf.

Relatives and legal representatives on behalf of a dead person.

A local councillor can act on behalf of a complainant, provided the complainant consents. But one local authority cannot complain about another local authority and individual local councillors cannot complain about the decisions of their own authority in their capacity as members.

Cost

Free to complainants.

Geographical limits

Complaints must be against the authorities in Wales listed on the previous page.

There is no restriction on the complainant's place of residence.

Time limits

Complaints must usually be made within 12 months of the day on which the complainant was first aware of the problem.

The Ombudsman can investigate a complaint made after the 12-month limit if he considers it reasonable to do so.

Remedies

There is no restriction on the form of redress the Ombudsman can recommend, provided it is within the legal powers of the authority concerned.

Financial compensation

There is no maximum on the amount the Ombudsman can recommend. Can include compensation for actual financial loss, distress and inconvenience. For loss, the highest actual award in 1995/96 was £20,150. For distress and inconvenience, the highest actual award was £500.

May recommend interest be paid on compensation if complainants have been deprived of something to which they were entitled (for example, a grant) for an unreasonable period.

May sometimes recommend that the authority concerned pays the complainant's costs, providing they were incurred because of the authority's maladministration.

May occasionally reduce the amount of compensation if the actions of the complainant or those acting on his or her behalf contributed to the problem.

Other

Can recommend any corrective action that would be a suitable remedy for the injustice to the complainant even an apology.

2. The complaints procedure

Making the complaint

Complainants can approach the scheme direct. Complaints must be in writing. A standard complaints form is available in the scheme leaflet, but not compulsory. If complainants have difficulty completing the form, an investigator calls on them to help complete it.

Exhausting the internal complaints procedure

Complainants do not have to exhaust internal channels of complaint before they approach the Ombudsman scheme. However, before it investigates, the scheme sends the complaint to the authority concerned for a response, possible settlement and a request for information.

Powers of investigation

Power to call and examine witnesses, and to require the production of documents. People who try to obstruct an investigation can be held in contempt.

Criteria for decisions

Whether there has been maladministration in the way a decision has been reached which has caused injustice to the complainant, taking into account the law, good practice and what is fair and reasonable.

Aims to be consistent with previous rulings.

Confidentiality

All formal reports on full investigations are sent to the media: they do not contain anything which would enable the complainant to be identified, but the name of the authority concerned is published. In exceptional cases (for instance, involving abuse of children) an order may be given not to publish the formal report at all. The authority concerned must also put a notice in the press, announcing that the report is available for public inspection.

Information obtained in the course of an investigation must not be disclosed except in the Ombudsman's report or to enable him to explain his reasons for a decision. In practice, most of the information obtained is usually disclosed in the formal report or decision letter so that the reasons for the decision can be understood. Exceptions include, for example, confidential social services information.

Summaries of all cases (naming the authorities concerned, but not the complainants) appear in the *Annual Report*.

Stages in complaint resolution

Screening

A complaint is first screened to see whether it is within the Ombudsman's jurisdiction. Cases that are not eligible are, where possible, automatically forwarded to another appropriate complaints-handling body.

Preliminary investigation

If the complaint is within the scheme's remit and there is some evidence of maladministration or injustice, it undergoes preliminary investigation. The complaint is sent to the authority concerned with a request for relevant information and the authority's comments. Authorities are asked for an initial response within 3 weeks, although many ask for an extension and this is normally agreed, particularly where the issues are complex. Sometimes written evidence is sufficient at this stage, but site visits and interviews may be necessary (hearings involving both parties to the complaint are not held). The authority is given an opportunity, and where appropriate encouraged, to settle the complaint at this stage. If the complaint remains unsettled, the Ombudsman will consider the authority's response and any other information.

If it is considered that the complaint cannot or should not be investigated further, a preliminary decision letter is issued.

Full investigation

If it is considered that there is a case to answer, and a need to issue a public report, a full investigation, including interviews, site visits and the examination of files, is carried out.

Draft report

Following a full investigation, a draft report (excluding conclusions) is sent to the complainant, the authority and all those interviewed. Its purpose is to verify the factual part of the report before conclusions are added, but both parties may also submit comments and points for consideration.

Final report

The Ombudsman's final report is then issued. It is made public and sent to the press.

Further report

If the Ombudsman is not satisfied with the authority's response to his final report, he may issue a further report.

Progress reports

Complainants are informed of the progress of their complaint from time to time as necessary, and at each stage in the process.

Types of ruling

Negotiation and informal conciliation

22% of cases were dealt with in this way in 1996/97.

Formal report

6% of cases were dealt with in this way in 1996/97.

The majority of cases - 94% in 1996/97 - are not the subject of a public report because the complaint has been settled without the need for such a report, or it is not within the scheme's remit, there is no evidence of maladministration and injustice, or there would be no purpose in pursuing it - for example, because the authority concerned has already issued an apology for a minor administrative failure.

Rights of appeal against a decision

The Ombudsman is not obliged to reconsider a decision not to pursue enquiries beyond the preliminary stage, but in practice he is prepared to do so. Once he has issued a formal public report he cannot re-open the matter.

There is no right of appeal to an outside body, except through judicial review in the High Court (there have been 2 applications for judicial review in 5 years: neither was successful).

The Ombudsman cannot refer points of law to the courts for a decision.

Failure to comply with rulings

Failure of an authority to comply with a recommendation

This happens in less than 1% of cases. The Ombudsman issues a further report.

Failure of an authority to comply with a further report

The Ombudsman can require the authority to publish a statement in the press at its own expense (a sanction so far imposed 3 times).

How long does the process take?

Target timescale

In 1996 - 10 weeks for preliminary decisions, 45 weeks for the issue of a final report.

Actual timescale

In 1996 - 10 weeks for preliminary decisions, 37 weeks for the issue of a final report.

For urgent cases (for example, complaints about school admission decisions in August when the school year starts in September), the Ombudsman tries to reach a decision quickly.

Sometimes a telephone call to the authority concerned may resolve a simple issue without the need for correspondence.

Delegation of decision-making

The Ombudsman has delegated to the secretary of the scheme the power to make all decisions on his behalf except for the issue of a formal public report on a full and formal investigation into a complaint. The Ombudsman signs every formal public report. Decision letters after preliminary investigation are signed either by the Ombudsman personally or by the secretary to the scheme.

Following up complaints

Cases not within the scheme's remit are not followed up.

When the Ombudsman has issued a formal report, the authority concerned is required by law to let him know within 3 months whether it has complied with his recommendations.

Complaining about the scheme itself

Complaints about the scheme are dealt with either by the Ombudsman or the secretary to the Commission. (Statistics are not available.)

3. The scheme's structure and administration

Origins and membership

A statutory scheme set up by the Local Government Act 1974 (as subsequently amended) and, by law, covering all the authorities listed above (see Service-providers covered). Started operating in 1974.

Structure and accountability

There is no body responsible for overseeing the work of the Commission. The Ombudsman is financially accountable through the Welsh Office to the Public Accounts Committee of the House of Commons.

The Ombudsman

Appointment

By the Queen, on the recommendation of the Secretary of State for Wales. Can be removed on grounds of incapacity or misbehaviour.

Term of appointment

No maximum, but must retire at 65.

Role

Overall responsibility for running the Commission and for the investigation of complaints.

Scheme's terms of reference

Set out in the Local Government Act 1974. Can only be changed by amending legislation.

Monitoring

Standards of service are published in the *Annual Report*.

BIOA member?

Yes.

Funding

Through the revenue support grant provided by central government for local government in Wales.

Costs

Running cost

£588,160 in 1996/97 (£555,357 in 1995/96).

Cost per complaint

£608 in 1996/97 (£520 in 1995/96).

Staffing

Overall responsibility

The Ombudsman. The head of staff is the secretary to the Commission.

Staff

6 investigators (or full-time equivalents), one of whom acts as office manager, and 1 assistant. (3 are solicitors who have some experience of local government.) 5 administrative staff.

Forthcoming changes

The Welsh Office is looking at the implications of the Department of Environment review of the Commission in England, particularly in respect of the Commission's organisation and jurisdiction.

Improving best practice

The Ombudsman can issue advice to authorities covered by the scheme. In recent years he has issued a good practice booklet and guidance in letters to chief executives, made specific reference to issues in the *Annual Report*, and made recommendations to the Welsh Office which has subsequently incorporated them in circulars to local authorities.

Facts and figures

Complaints determined [1]

Subject of complaint	1994/95	1995/96	% change
Building regulations	5	10	100.0
Education	21	73	248.0
Environmental health	56	53	-5.3
Council tax/rates	71	53	-25.3
General administration	6	12	100.0
Highways	85	93	9.4
Housing	321	321	0.0
Land transactions	33	43	30.3
Leisure	4	10	150.0
Licensing	15	7	-53.3
Miscellaneous	31	25	-19.3
Planning	349	267	-23.5
Social Services	31	62	100.0

[1] Statistics are not readily available for complaints received.

Complaints at each stage of procedure

	1994/95	1995/96	% change
Total complaints handled	1,028	1,030	0.2
Complaints sent back to internal procedures	1	0	- [1]
Complaints not within remit/referred elsewhere	55	37	-33.0
Complaints not pursued for other reasons	217	214	-1.4
Complaints reaching the next stage (ie. preliminary enquiries)	755	779	3.2
Complaints reaching the final stage (ie. issue of formal public report)	41	48	17.0

Outcome of complaints fully investigated

	1994/95	1995/96	% change
Complaint upheld	30 (73%)	34 (71%)	13.0
Complaint upheld in part	6	8	33.0
Complaint not upheld	2	4	100.0
Complaints discontinued because settled	3	2	-33.0

[1] Too small for percentage to be significant.

Information available about the scheme

Publicising the scheme

Leaflets about the scheme are held by local authorities and advice agencies.

The Ombudsman gives TV and radio interviews and talks to groups. Reports are circulated to the media.

Terms of reference

Published in the scheme's leaflet and *Annual Report*.

Annual Report

Published in June or July. In addition to the tables above, includes breakdowns of complaints in relation to each authority, complaints not accepted for full investigation, list of reports, balance sheet and revenue accounts.

Other publications

Evidence to the House of Commons Welsh Affairs Committee in November 1996 'Minutes of Evidence - The Commission for Local Administration in Wales', session 1996/97.

E.B.C. Osmotherly (editor), *Guide to the Local Government Ombudsman Service*, Pitman Publishing, 1995.

Evidence to the House of Commons Public Accounts Committee 'The Allocation of Housing' Development Board for Rural Wales, 23rd Report, session 1993/94.

Evidence to the House of Commons Welsh Affairs Committee in June 1993 'Rural Housing', Third Report, session 1992/93.

Welsh Commission, *Guidance on Complaints Systems*, June 1992.

Guidance notes for organisations covered by the scheme are also published.

Pensions Ombudsman

6th Floor, 11 Belgrave Road, London SW1V 1RB
Tel: 0171 834 9144. Fax: 0171 821 0065

Ombudsman: Dr Julian Farrand

1. Using the scheme: key points

Service-providers covered

By law, all occupational pension schemes, including those run by insurance companies for employers and trustees. Also covers personal pension plans, but in practice virtually all personal pension complaints are dealt with by other bodies - usually the Personal Investment Authority Ombudsman (see separate entry on page 177).

Complaints covered

Complaints by individuals of injustice caused by maladministration (or administrative failures). Complaints about maladministration made by a pension scheme's trustees, managers or an employer, do not need to allege injustice has been caused.

Disputes on a matter of fact or a point of law between the complainant and either the pension scheme trustees, the managers, or the employer.

Complaints not covered

Complaints about state pensions.

Complaints that have been, or can be, dealt with by one of the various investment and financial regulatory bodies or Ombudsmen. In particular:

- complaints about the selling of a personal pension are handled by the Personal Investment Authority Ombudsman;

- complaints about the administration of a personal pension are only handled by the Pensions Ombudsman if they are not within the remit of any other Ombudsman.

From 6 April 1997, complaints about non-compliance with a number of statutory rules must initially be handled by the Occupational Pensions Regulatory Authority (Invicta House, Trafalgar Place, Brighton BN1 4DW. Tel: 01273 627600).

Complaints where the circumstances persuade the Ombudsman that an investigation would be inappropriate or unjustifiable.

Cases on which a court or tribunal has already ruled or where court or tribunal proceedings have already begun.

Who can complain?

A member or a prospective member of the pension scheme in question. 'Members' include:

- anyone claiming to be, or entitled to be, a member;

- anyone with pensionable service who has left the pension scheme before retirement age.

A widow, widower or surviving dependant of a pension scheme member who has died.

A relative or other suitable representative, if a person in the categories above is unable to look after his or her own affairs.

The trustees or managers of a scheme can complain about the employer's actions, and the employer about the trustees' or manager's actions. Trustees and managers can also complain about any trustee or manager of another scheme.

Cost

Free to complainants.

Geographical limits

Complaints must concern pension schemes in the legal jurisdiction of England, Wales, Scotland, Northern Ireland and the Isle of Man.

There are no restrictions on the nationality or place of residence of the complainant.

Time limits

Complaints must be brought within 3 years of the act or omission that caused the problem. If the complainant did not know about the matter at the time, the 3 years start from the time he or she could reasonably be expected to have known about it.

The Ombudsman can deal with complaints outside this time limit where he considers it reasonable to do so. From 6 April 1997, he does not count in the 3 years any time spent in the internal complaints procedure and the Pensions Advisory Service (see Exhausting the internal complaints procedure below).

Remedies

Financial

Can make an award for financial loss. There is no formal maximum amount. In 1995/96, excluding one particularly large case, the highest actual award for financial loss for one individual was £124,000 - but the Ombudsman's office does not always know the exact amount of an award if, for instance, it awards the transfer value of a pension.

Can make an award for distress, delay and inconvenience. (The average award for distress, delay and inconvenience in 1995/96 was £500, and the highest was £5,000.)

Can order the payment of interest on an award, where payment has been delayed.

Occasionally orders the pension scheme to pay the complainant's legal or other expert costs.

Other

The Ombudsman can recommend corrective action such as giving directions to put complainants in the position they should have been in.

He can also order a pension scheme to take corrective action that will benefit all the scheme members affected by one of his decisions (for example, to restore a trust fund) and can recommend a pension scheme makes an apology.

2. The complaints procedure

Making the complaint

Complainants can approach the Ombudsman direct. Complaints must be in writing, using the standard complaint form (there is a guidance leaflet). Complainants can get someone else (like a solicitor, accountant or trade union representative) to write for them, so long as they give that person written authority.

Exhausting the internal complaints procedure

Before the Ombudsman can deal with a complaint, complainants must have exhausted any internal complaints procedure and (unless they already have a professional adviser like a solicitor) are usually also expected to have used OPAS (the Pensions Advisory Service, 11 Belgrave Road, London SW1V 1RB. Tel: 0171 233 8080). OPAS is an independent voluntary organisation with local advisers, experienced in pension matters, who will attempt to conciliate, where appropriate.

From 6 April 1997 most pension schemes must have their own internal disputes resolution procedures. The Ombudsman is prohibited from investigating a complaint until the pension scheme has issued a written notice of its final internal decision. However, he can investigate if there seems to be no real prospect of such a notice being issued.

Powers of investigation

Has the right to compel the disclosure of all relevant information from any source. If the Ombudsman holds a hearing, attendance is not compulsory, although he does have power to compel witnesses to appear if he thinks it necessary.

Criteria for decisions

The rules and regulations of the pension scheme concerned and whether they have been followed correctly, within the legal framework of statute and trust law and in accordance with good practice.

Previous decisions of the Ombudsman are not binding, although in practice decisions in very similar cases are taken into account and usually followed. If there has been an appeal through the courts against a decision by the Ombudsman, this is treated as a binding precedent.

Confidentiality

During the investigation, copies of all correspondence and documentation are sent to all parties involved.

The *Annual Report* gives a digest of most cases, without identifying the complainants or the pension schemes concerned.

The Ombudsman allows selected bodies to publish his decisions, either edited or in full. The names of the parties are not necessarily omitted.

Stages in complaint resolution

New complaints

The new complaints team considers the complaint form and decides if there are sufficient details to accept or reject the complaint. Problems are discussed with the casework director or the Ombudsman. If necessary, extra details or a statement from the complainant are obtained. If the complaint is accepted, the investigation team leader will consider whether special investigation expertise is needed and allocate the case to an investigator.

The new complaints team may decide (if necessary, after discussion with the casework director) to refer the complaint to OPAS or some other body. If the complaint concerns a personal pension, the complainant is referred to the Personal Investment Authority Ombudsman. In other instances, the case may be rejected as out of the Ombudsman's remit, out of time or unsuitable or inappropriate for investigation.

Fast-track procedure

This is used when it is unlikely the Ombudsman will uphold the complaint. A letter explaining why is sent to the complainant. The complainant's response is considered and, on the basis of this response, either the case is accepted for full investigation or a letter of determination against the complainant is drafted (called a 'short decision'), then approved and signed by the Ombudsman.

Full investigation

If a case is accepted for full investigation, the investigator sends the complaint details and other documentation to anybody against whom allegations are made, inviting comments and explaining the scope of the investigation. Responses are considered and further information sought as necessary. Hearings may be held to resolve disputed facts: they are held at the Ombudsman's office. The scheme may meet the complainant's expenses (but not those of any professional adviser). The investigator then drafts a provisional determination. When approved by the Ombudsman, the provisional determination is sent to all parties concerned for comments. The responses are considered and, in the light of these, the determination is finalised. It is then approved and signed by the Ombudsman.

Progress reports

Only issued where a lengthy delay is expected - for example if there are a number of cases of the same kind about the same pension scheme, and only one case is being actively investigated.

Types of ruling

Full determination

Made after a full investigation. This is a final decision and is binding on both the complainant and those responsible for the management of the pension scheme. (The Ombudsman makes a determination in most completed cases.)

Short decision

Made after a fast-track investigation in a small number of cases which clearly cannot be settled in the complainant's favour (28 cases in 1995/96). This is binding in the same way as a full determination.

Rights of appeal against a decision

There is no right to ask the Ombudsman to reconsider his decision. (In practice, the provisional determination issued to all parties gives them a last chance to argue for a different result.)

Once the Ombudsman has issued a final decision (or determination), there is a right of appeal, on a point of law only, to the High Court (in Scotland the Court of Session or in Northern Ireland the Court of Appeal). (There have been 55 such appeals in the scheme's lifetime, out of more than 900 decisions.)

It is not yet established whether the scheme is subject to judicial review.

The Ombudsman can refer a particular question to the courts to resolve an important point of law although this has never been done.

The way a complaint has been handled by the Ombudsman can be investigated by the Parliamentary Ombudsman, though not the decision itself.

Failure to comply with rulings

Complainants can enforce a ruling by the Pensions Ombudsman through the county court (in Scotland, through the Sheriff). (Enforcement has been necessary in some cases.)

How long does the process take?

Target timescale

As an average for completed cases, no more than 12 months from the time a complaint is accepted for investigation.

Actual timescales

In 1995/96: 37% of determinations were completed in 6 months or less, 33% in 7 to 12 months, 10% in 13 to 18 months; the remaining 20% took longer than 18 months.

Delegation of decision-making

There is no Deputy Ombudsman, and the Ombudsman's powers to decide on complaints cannot be delegated in any way. He approves all provisional and signs all final determinations.

Following up complaints

The scheme does not monitor the outcomes of decisions or complaints not within its jurisdiction.

Complaining about the scheme itself

Complaints about the scheme's service are usually dealt with at a senior level and not by any member of staff against whom the complaint was made. Complaints can also be referred to the Parliamentary Ombudsman.

3. The scheme's structure and administration

Origins and membership

A statutory scheme, now governed by the Pension Schemes Act 1993, as amended by the Pensions Act 1995. Started operating on 1 April 1991 under previous pensions legislation.

Structure and accountability

The Pensions Ombudsman scheme is overseen by the Secretary of State for Social Security. The

Ombudsman is completely independent in his quasi-judicial capacity and his independence is set out in the legislation.

The Ombudsman

Appointment

By the Secretary of State for Social Security, who has the power of dismissal on 6 months notice (no dismissal grounds required).

Term of appointment

Initially 5 years, no limits on re-appointment.

Role

Making the final decisions on complaints, responsible for the running of the office, but day-to-day management is devolved to a management team.

Scheme's terms of reference

These are laid down in the Pensions Act 1993 as amended in 1995. Can only be changed by amending legislation.

Monitoring

A charter statement of service aims is published in the *Annual Report*.

BIOA member?

Yes.

Funding

Funding comes from a levy on occupational pension schemes, collected by the Occupational Pensions Board. This is channelled via the Department of Social Security, which makes up any shortfall to the level required for the Ombudsman to operate efficiently.

Costs

Running cost

£1.18 million in 1995/96 (£1.058 million in 1994/95).

Cost per complaint

Not published.

Staffing

Overall responsibility

The scheme's administrator.

Staff

Currently 17 casework staff (including 2 part-time) and 8 administrative staff. Casework staff are recruited mainly from the pensions industry. An in-house litigation solicitor is also retained.

Forthcoming changes

None.

Improving best practice

No specific powers, but the Ombudsman draws attention to best practice by establishing a high profile for his office through articles, speaking engagements, and so on.

Facts and figures

Numbers of complaints resolved[1]

Subject of complaint	1995/96
Contribution refunds and queries	10
Transfers	30
Preserved pension requirements	4
Membership conditions	12
Enhancement of pensions	9
Early retirement	12
Ill-health benefits	21
Spouse's and dependant's benefits	14
Additional voluntary contributions	4
Incorrect/late or no payments	23
No response from scheme	3
Winding up of scheme	34
Use of pension fund surplus	11
Disclosure of information	11
Calculation of benefits	22
Other matters	21

[1] 'Bulk' complaints (those where a large number of individuals complain about one particular problem with one scheme) are classed as one complaint.

Numbers of complaints at each stage of procedure

	1994/95	1995/96	% change
Total new cases received	2,186	3,639	66.00
Referred to OPAS	846	1,324	56.50
Not acceptable for investigation	1,002	1,140	13.80
Case abandoned	N/A	299	-
New casework	353	829	135.00
Investigations discontinued (eg. settled)	54	47	-12.96

Outcome of cases completed

	1994/95	1995/96
'Fast track' decisions against the complainant	7 (8%)	28 (8%)
Determinations wholly or partly in the complainant's favour	65 (78%)	241 (68%)[1]
Determinations not in the complainant's favour	11 (13%)	85 (24%)

[1] Includes 87 cases involved in two large 'bulk' complaints, all of which were successful.

Information available about the scheme

Publicising the scheme

Occupational pension schemes must, by law, inform their members of the existence of the Ombudsman. Since 6 April 1997 they have also had a duty to inform each individual complainant, as part of their own internal complaints procedure.

To publicise the scheme, the Ombudsman uses the *Annual Report* and press conference, gives speeches, write articles, and is interviewed by the press and others. He is considering publishing a regular digest of cases (rather than including them in the *Annual Report*).

A scheme booklet is available from the Ombudsman.

Terms of reference

Published in the Pensions Act 1993 (as amended in 1995), and regulations thereunder, and summarised in the scheme booklet.

Annual Report

Published in July or August. In addition to the tables above, includes some historical information on the outcome of complaints and time taken to resolve them, further information on caseflows and expenditure.

Other publications

J.T. Farrand, 'Farrand's First Year', *Pensions Management* (also published in *Pension Funds and Their Advisers*), 1996.

J.T. Farrand, 'Jurisdiction to deal with pensions complaints in the light of the Pensions Act', *Journal of Pensions Management*, December 1996.

J.T. Farrand, 'Pensions Ombudsman v Courts', *Journal of the Association of Pensions Lawyers*, 1995.

Prisons Ombudsman

St Vincent House, 30 Orange Street, London WC2 7HH
Tel: 0171 389 1527. Fax: 0171 389 1492

Ombudsman: Sir Peter Woodhead

1. Using the scheme: key points

Service-providers covered

Prisons in England and Wales, including contracted-out prisons, contracted-out services and the actions of people working in prisons but not employed by the Prison Service.

Prison Service headquarters.

Complaints covered

Complaints from prisoners who have failed to obtain satisfaction from the prison service's requests and complaints system about, for example, their property, transfer or allocation, temporary release, disciplinary adjudications or general conditions.

Complaints not covered

Ministerial decisions.

Complaints where the Ombudsman considers that no worthwhile outcome can be achieved and no substantial issues are raised.

Complaints about decisions involving the clinical judgment of doctors.

Cases already subject to court proceedings or, usually, on which a court has already ruled. If court action is imminent or likely, the Ombudsman would postpone dealing with the complaint.

Who can complain?

Individual prisoners.

Legal representatives or MPs on a prisoner's behalf, with the consent of the prisoner.

Cost

Free to complainants.

Geographical limits

The complaint must be about treatment in a prison in England or Wales.

Time limits

Complaints must be made to the Ombudsman within 1 month of receiving a final reply about the complaint from the prison service.

The Ombudsman will not usually accept a complaint if there has been a delay of more than 12 months between the prisoner becoming aware of the relevant facts and submitting a complaint to the scheme, unless the delay has been the fault of the prison service.

The Ombudsman can consider complaints outside these time limits if he considers there is a good reason for the delay or where the issues raised are so serious as to override the time factor.

Remedies

Financial compensation

Compensation can be recommended for actual loss or damage - for example, loss of property or physical injury. The Ombudsman has not recommended financial redress for other matters, although there is no actual prohibition. There is no maximum amount. (Average actual award: between £30 and £80; highest actual award to date: £1,100.)

Can order the payment of interest on an award or the costs of legal or other expert advice to either party (but has never done so in practice).

Has wide discretion to reduce the size of an award, if the actions of the complainant have contributed to the problem.

Other

> The Ombudsman can recommend corrective action, for example: transfer to another prison; quashing disciplinary findings; or punishments. He can also recommend the review of a policy or procedure, and that an apology be made.

2. The complaints procedure

Making the complaint

> Complainants can approach the scheme direct (but see Exhausting the internal complaints procedure below). Complaints must be in writing except in urgent and exceptional cases. There is no standard form, but a guidance leaflet is available: the leaflet is available in 10 languages and there is a translation service so that prisoners may write in their first language.

Exhausting the internal complaints procedure

> The complainant must first exhaust all internal channels of complaint and a formal answer to a prisoner's request/complaint must have been received. This requirement can be waived if the prison service fails to complete processing of an appeal within 6 weeks.

Powers of investigation

> Has unfettered access to prison service documents relevant to complaints and can visit prisons to interview employees, prisoners and others. Cannot compel individuals to attend hearings or respond to enquiries.

Criteria for decisions

> Can consider both the merits of the case and the procedures followed. In practice, emphasis is placed on whether the manner in which the prisoner was treated was just, reasonable and in accordance with the wider demands of law and the public good, as well as on whether the prison

service has complied with its own rules and procedures.

For complaints concerning disciplinary adjudications, the Ombudsman also takes into account the high standard of proof required for these quasi-judicial processes (that is, the test of guilt beyond reasonable doubt).

The Ombudsman aims to be consistent but is not bound by his previous decisions.

Confidentiality

To help decide whether a complaint is within jurisdiction, the Ombudsman will tell the prison service the nature of the complaint, revealing the complainant's name, and, where necessary, the prison service will then provide the Ombudsman with relevant information.

Noteworthy cases are published in the *Annual Report* - neither the prisoner nor the prison concerned is usually identified, but the Ombudsman will usually identify the type of prisoner held, for example by his or her category. Information that might compromise security, put a third party at risk, or damage a prisoner's health is not published. It is open to the complainant to publish the Ombudsman's findings.

Stages in complaint resolution

Eligibility

When a letter is received from the complainant, the details are entered on computer (by an administrative assistant) who then passes the complaint to an administrative officer. To decide whether the complaint is eligible, enquiries may need to be made with prisons, prison service headquarters, etc. If the complaint is eligible, the administrative officer passes the details to the investigating officer.

If the complaint is not eligible, the administrative officer writes explaining why: the complainant may be referred to other agencies able to help (such as the Prisoners' Advice Service or the Prison Reform Trust).

Investigation

The investigating officer writes to the prisoner saying the case has been accepted, asking for relevant documents and information, and setting out a timetable. The investigating officer gathers all the relevant information by writing, telephoning and interviewing (hearings are not held). He/she researches the relevant rules and procedures and, after consideration, writes up the first draft report (the aim is to complete this within 8 weeks of accepting the complaint).

Draft report

An Assistant Ombudsman considers the complaint, seeks further information and re-drafts the report as necessary. He/she makes a proposal whether to uphold or reject the complaint. The Ombudsman considers the draft report. When agreed, the draft report is sent to the director general of the prison service, who has 7 days to check it for security or disclosure issues. The report may be amended in the light of prison service comments. The prison service and the complainant then have 7 days to comment on the facts.

Final report

Any comments received on the draft report are considered by the investigating officer, the Assistant Ombudsman and the Ombudsman. The final report is then signed by the Ombudsman. Copies are sent to the complainant and the prison service.

Final reply

The prison service has 6 weeks within which to accept or reject any recommendations in the final report. Following this, the prison service's final reply is sent to the complainant.

Progress reports

Complainants are informed at the outset that the aim is to complete the investigation within 12 weeks. The complainant gets the draft report for factual checking (after about 10 weeks). If the process is taking longer, the complainant is kept informed of progress on a monthly basis.

Types of ruling

Final report

Issued in all cases that are investigated.

Non-binding recommendation

Made, if at all, in the final report (a recommendation is not binding on either party).

Rights of appeal against a decision

Neither party has any right to require the Ombudsman to reconsider his final decision or to appeal against his decision.

The complainant retains the right to take a case to court or complain to the Parliamentary Ombudsman (see separate entry on page 69).

The scheme is subject to judicial review (there have been none so far).

The Ombudsman cannot refer particular questions to a court to resolve a point of law.

Failure to comply with rulings

The Ombudsman has no powers or sanctions to enforce his recommendations. (Over a period of 14 months the prison service failed to comply in 20 cases or 10% of all complaints investigated.)

How long does the process take?

Target timescale

12 weeks from acceptance of the complaint to completion.

Actual timescale

11 weeks average.

The Ombudsman will deal with a case quickly if it is a matter of urgency (such as an appeal against an adjudication for which the prisoner is already serving added days).

Delegation of decision-making

The Ombudsman's powers are not delegated, except to an Assistant Ombudsman in his absence. The Ombudsman sees and approves all cases and signs every decision letter.

Following up complaints

Complaints are not followed up if they are outside the scheme's remit or not accepted because they are still in the prison's internal complaints system. However, the complainants outside the remit will be advised of other avenues of redress where they exist.

The Ombudsman monitors compliance with decisions only in that he asks complainants to get back to him if a recommendation which has been accepted by the authority concerned has not been implemented.

Complaining about the scheme itself

There is no formal procedure (and no record of how many such complaints have been received).

3. The scheme's structure and administration

Origins and membership

The scheme was established following the Woolf report into the 1990 prison riots. Its status and terms of reference are established under non-statutory terms of reference set by the Home Secretary. It started operating in October 1994.

Structure and accountability

The Prisons Ombudsman is independent of the Prison Service Agency but reports directly to the Home Secretary (to whom the Agency is also accountable). Disagreements about the scheme's remit between the prison service and the Ombudsman are decided by the Home Secretary.

The Ombudsman

Appointment

By the Home Secretary. The usual civil service rules on dismissal apply.

Term of appointment

Initially 3 years, extendable to 5. No restrictions on reappointment.

Role

Overall responsibility for running the scheme and handling complaints.

Scheme's terms of reference

These were originally given in two documents from the prison service (*A Proposal for Ministerial Consideration,* 1992 and a *Note of Arrangements for the Establishment of the Post*, April 1994). The terms of reference are now in a document issued by the Home Secretary in May 1996. The terms of reference can be changed by the Home Secretary at his discretion.

Monitoring

Standards of service are published in the Annual Report.

BIOA member?

No.

Funding

Comes directly from the Home Office.

Costs

Running cost

£661,607 for 14 months from October 1994 to December 1995 (excluding start-up capital costs).

Cost per complaint

£323 (excluding start-up capital costs).

Staffing

Overall responsibility

The Ombudsman.

Assistant Ombudsmen

There are 3 Assistant Ombudsmen (appointed in a similar way to the Ombudsman) - one is legally qualified, one previously worked in a prisoner pressure group, one is a career civil servant whose last post was in the prison service. The Assistant Ombudsmen supervise the investigating officers and provide draft reports, managerial support and legal advice.

Staff

9 investigating officers and 5 administrative staff. All staff other than the 3 Assistant Ombudsmen are Home Office civil servants with general administrative backgrounds. One is a seconded prison governor.

Occasionally the Ombudsman seeks the help of members of the prison's board of visitors (the lay watchdogs for individual prisons) in investigating a complaint.

Forthcoming changes

No changes planned.

Improving best practice

The Ombudsman has no powers to promote best practice, other than by persuasion, visits to prison establishments and through his Annual Report.

Facts and figures

Numbers of new complaints received in writing (including ineligible complaints)

Subject of complaint	14 months to 31/12/95	1/1/96 to 31/12/96
Disciplinary adjudications	206	273
Assaults	57	51
Security/categorisation	145	147
Food	30	19
General conditions	214	211
Regime activities	62	109
Links - visits, telephone calls etc.	107	118
Medical	56	53
Temporary release	283	147
Property	361	272
Race	19	15
Segregation in prison	49	26
Transfer/allocation to particular prisons	304	238
Miscellaneous	115	81

Numbers of complaints at each stage of procedure

	14 months to 31/12/95	1/1/96 to 31/12/96
Complaints not within remit/referred elsewhere	1,368 [1]	1,304 [2]
Complaints not pursued for other reasons	98	64
Complaints investigated	424	499
Final reports issued	424	445
Total complaints handled	2,050	1,897

Outcome of complaints fully investigated

Complaint upheld/upheld in part	187	186
Complaint not upheld	237	259

[1] Most of these had not completed the internal complaints system.

Information available about the scheme

Publicising the scheme

The terms of reference state that prisoners should have confidential access to the scheme and that prison service staff will not seek to prevent a prisoner from referring a complaint to the Ombudsman.

Governors of prisons are instructed to make information leaflets, videos and audiotapes about the Ombudsman's work widely available to prisoners. Information is also given in a *Prisoner Information Book* issued to all prisoners.

Terms of reference

Available at all prisons and on request, and will be published in the 1996 *Annual Report*.

Annual Report

The 1995 report was published in October 1996. (It covers the calendar year 1995.) In addition to the tables above it includes monthly breakdowns of complaints received, some information on the type of complainant, further information on eligibility, prison service responses and response time, complaints upheld by month and category, types of recommendation, and some further financial information.

Other publications

Select Committee on the Parliamentary Commission for Administration, Fourth Report, *Report of the Parliamentary Ombudsman for 1995 - 380* (including 330-i of Session 1995-96).

The Scottish Prisons Complaints Commission

Saughton House, Broomhouse Drive, Edinburgh, EH11 3XA
Tel: 0131 244 8423. Lo-call: 0345 023402
Fax: 0131 244 8430

Commissioner: Dr James McManus

1. Using the scheme: key points

Service-providers covered

Prisons in Scotland including all ancillary services (social work, education, medical, psychiatric) provided by the Scottish Prison Service.

Complaints covered

Complaints from prisoners who have failed to obtain satisfaction from the Scottish Prison Service complaints system about any matter under its control.

Complaints not covered

Complaints about medical, social work, psychological or related services involving professional judgement.

Complaints which are subject to legal action.

Complaints about conviction or sentence.

Complaints about parole board decisions and release on life licence.

Who can complain

Individual prisoners.

When anyone else complains on a prisoner's behalf, the Commission first checks with the prisoner involved that he/she wishes to proceed with the complaint.

Cost

Free to complainants.

Geographical limits

The complaint must be about matters within the jurisdiction of the Scottish Prison Service.

Time limits

Complaints must be made to the Commission within 3 months of receiving a final reply from the Scottish Prison Service.

Remedies

Financial compensation

Usually confined to cases involving compensation for actual loss or damage to property. There is no limit on the amount that can be awarded.

Other

The Ombudsman can recommend corrective action which might include quashing of disciplinary findings, or a review of policy or procedure. He can also recommend issuing an apology and/or explanation.

2. The complaints procedure

Making the complaint

Complainants must submit applications in writing. There is a standard form but it is not compulsory. Letters to and from the Commissioner are not subject to censorship by the prison. An information leaflet is available in all prisons. Prisoners may telephone the Commission on an 0345 number at local call charges: help can be provided to put the complaint in writing.

Exhausting the internal complaints procedure

Complainants must first exhaust all the relevant parts of the Scottish Prison Service complaints system. If this procedure fails to produce replies within the timescales laid down in Prison Rules, the Commission has immediate jurisdiction.

Powers of investigation

Unfettered access to Scottish Prison Service documents, establishments, personnel and prisoners. Cannot compel other individuals to respond to enquiries.

Criteria for decisions

Can consider both the merits of the case and the procedures followed. In practice, emphasis is placed on whether the manner in which the complainant was treated was just, reasonable and fair.

The Prisons Act 1989 (as amended), Prison Rules, and normal administrative law procedures. The Commission looks for compliance with the spirit of the law, and of international law, as well as with the letter of the law. It also aims to promote good practice.

Confidentiality

All correspondence between prisoners and the Commission is confidential. Letters to and from the Commission are not subject to censorship in any way.

The Commission tries, where possible, to maintain the confidentiality of its proceedings. When an investigation requires access to more than individual files, it is often not possible to maintain the anonymity of the complainant.

The findings of the Commission in individual cases are reported only to the complainant and to the chief executive of the Scottish Prison Service. The complainant may choose to publish the Commission's findings.

The *Annual Report* contains summaries of many cases in anonymous form.

Stages in complaint resolution

Eligibility

All applications are acknowledged within 5 days and an immediate check is made to find whether the applicant has exhausted the internal complaints procedure. Ineligible complaints are returned to the applicant with an explanation of the action required to further the complaint.

Investigation

The Commissioner investigates all cases personally, usually by visiting the prison where the applicant is held and consulting relevant prison files. Some of this work can be done by writing and telephoning though much of it needs to be done on the spot.

Conciliation

It is possible in many cases to conciliate the matter within the prison and agree on a course of action which the complainant accepts as a method of resolving the grievance.

Report

Whether or not a complaint is resolved by conciliation, a report is prepared for the applicant detailing the Commission's findings and conclusion. If the conclusion involves a formal recommendation to the chief executive, this letter is copied to the chief executive of the Scottish Prison Service.

Reply

The chief executive's reply to formal recommendations is immediately copied to the complainant.

Types of ruling

Conciliation

When a conciliated settlement has been reached, this is recorded in the final report and a copy of the report is sent to both the applicant and the member of staff who took part in the conciliation.

No recommendation

When the Commission concludes that no recommendation is required as a result of its investigation, this is recorded in the decision letter which is sent only to the applicant.

Formal recommendations

These are recorded in the final report to the applicant and copied to the Chief Executive of the Scottish Prison Service.

Rights of appeal against a decision

Neither party has any right to require the Commission to reconsider the final decision or to appeal against the decision.

Applicants retain the right to take cases to court and to complain to the Parliamentary Ombudsman (see separate entry on page 69).

The scheme is subject to judicial review, though there has not yet been one.

The Commission cannot refer particular questions to a court to resolve a point of law.

Failure to comply with rulings

The Commission has no powers to enforce its recommendations. In its first 2 years of operation some 4 recommendations were not acted upon by the chief executive of the Scottish Prison Service.

How long does the process take?

Target timescale

4 weeks from acceptance of the complaint to completion.

Actual timescale

12 working days in 1996.

Following up complaints

The Commission asks applicants to inform it if a recommendation which has been accepted is not implemented.

A sample of all complainants are issued with a questionnaire each year to give their views on the operation of the scheme and the impact of their complaint on them.

Complaining about the scheme itself

Apart from the sample who receive a questionnaire, there is no formal mechanism for complaining about the scheme itself.

3. The scheme's structure and administration

Origins and membership

The scheme was established following the Woolf Report into the 1990 prison riots and the commitment made in the Justice Charter for Scotland 1991. Its Terms of Reference are set by the Secretary of State for Scotland. The scheme started operating in December 1994.

Structure and accountability

The Scottish Prisons Complaints Commission is independent of the Scottish Prison Service and reports directly to the Secretary of State.

The Commissioner

Appointment

Under contract to the Secretary of State for Scotland. The usual civil service rules on dismissal apply.

Term of appointment

Initially 3 years extendible to 5.

Role

Overall responsibility for establishing and running the scheme, handling complaints and organising the budget.

Scheme's terms of reference

These are laid down in an annex to the Commissioner's contract.

Monitoring

The contract requires the Commissioner to submit an *Annual Report* to the Secretary of State for Scotland, and this is laid before Parliament and published.

BIOA member?

No.

Funding

Comes directly from the Scottish Office.

Costs

Running cost

£144,548 6 April 1995 to 5 April 1996.

Cost per complaint

£666 including start-up capital costs.

Staffing

The Commissioner and a personal secretary are the only staff in the office. There was initially a Deputy Commissioner but there was insufficient work to require that level of staffing.

Forthcoming changes

No changes planned.

Improving best practice

The Commissioner has no formal power to promote best practice but spends considerable time in discussion with prisoners and staff on matters arising in the course of investigations.

Facts and figures

Breakdown of cases by subject 1995

Subject	Total	Ineligible	Eligible	Rec made	No rec made
Security category	38	12	24	11	13
Visits	17	9	8	1	7
Downgrading	14	3	11	5	6
Property	15	8	7	3	4
Orderly room	27	7	18	11	7
Food	5	4	1	-	1
Mail	6	1	4	1	3
Transfers	11	6	5	2	3
Living environment	2	2	-	-	-
Home leave	5	3	2	1	1
Medical treatment	14	14	-	-	-
Protection	3	1	2	2	-
Location	2	2	-	-	-
Parole	2	-	2	-	2
Remission/ADA	3	-	3	-	2
Victimisation	5	2	3	-	3
Religion	1	1	-	-	-
Postage costs	2	-	2	-	2
Education	2	1	1	-	1
Work	4	2	2	2	-
Compensation	1	1	-	-	-
GP system	8	1	7	3	3
Liberation date	2	1	1	1	-
Treatment of member of staff	1	1	-	-	-
Security	2	1	1	-	1
Use of call button	3	-	3	-	3
Association	3	1	2	1	1
Social work	2	2	-	-	-
Urine testing	2	2	-	-	-
Telephone calls	1	-	1	-	1
Outside placement	2	-	2	1	1
Exercise	1	1	-	-	-
Access to media	1	-	1	-	1
Personal officer	1	1	-	-	-
Use of TV in cell	1	-	1	-	1
Miscellaneous	10	5	5	1	4

Number of complaints at each stage of procedure

	1995
Total initial complaints	217
Initial complaints sent back to internal procedures	83
Initial complaints not within remit/referred elsewhere	14
Initial complaints reaching the next stage in the complaints process	N/A
Complaints reaching the next stage in the complaints process	N/A
Complaints reaching the final stage in the complaints process	120

Outcome of complaints

Complaint upheld	41
Complaint rejected or other outcome	1
Complaint part accepted	4
Complaint accepted	36

Information available about the scheme

Publicising the scheme

The Commission publishes an information leaflet and provides supplies of these to each prison. Each prisoner should receive a copy on admission to the prison. In addition, posters have been provided to all penal establishments and are prominently displayed in prison halls. The Prisoner's Information Pack, published by the Scottish Prison Service, also contains full details of the Commission and how to access it.

Annual Report

The 1995 *Annual Report* was published in March 1996. It provided details of the procedure for bringing complaints to the Commission, a detailed breakdown on the number of complaints and the results of the Commission's investigations.

Police Complaints Authority

10 Great George Street, London SW1P 3AE
Tel: 0171 273 6450. Fax: 0171 273 6401

Chairman: Peter Moorhouse

1. Using the scheme: key points

Service-providers covered

All police forces in England and Wales.

The Ministry of Defence Police, British Transport Police and specialist forces covering the ports of Liverpool and Tilbury, the Royal Parks and the UK Atomic Energy Authority.

Complaints covered

Complaints concerning the quality of police service, including:

- incivility;

- failures in duty;

- assault;

- unlawful arrest or detention.

Complaints not covered

Complaints about the general administration, efficiency or procedures of a police force.

Complaints involving special constables, the civilian employees of a police force or any quasi-police forces that might be set up (for instance, by a local authority).

Complaints already subject to court proceedings or cases on which a court has already ruled, unless perjury is alleged.

Who can complain?

Private individuals or groups of people (but not businesses, charities or other unincorporated bodies).

Friends, relatives and legal representatives on behalf of an individual (provided they have written authorisation).

Friends, relatives and legal representatives on behalf of a dead person.

Cost

Free to complainants.

Geographical limits

The scheme covers police forces in England and Wales only.

Complainants do not have to be resident in England or Wales.

Time limits

Complaints usually have to reach the Authority within 12 months of the incident that gave rise to the complaint. This rule can be waived if there is good reason for the delay.

Remedies

Financial compensation

The Authority cannot award financial compensation: for this, the complainant has to bring a civil action for damages in court.

Other

The Authority can make recommendations, for example, a review of police force policy or disciplinary charges against the officer concerned. It can also recommend giving an explanation or apology.

2. The complaints procedure

Making the complaint

Applicants can complain directly to the Authority, or at a police station, or through the chief constable of the force concerned (in London, the Metropolitan Police Commissioner).

Complaints can be made in person or through a representative, like an MP.

Oral complaints are accepted, but the Authority will not take any action until it receives written confirmation. There is no standard complaint form, but there is a guidance leaflet.

Exhausting the internal complaints procedure

A complainant does not have to exhaust any internal police complaints procedures first, but the complaint must be recorded by the police force concerned before an investigation can begin. If, as sometimes happens, the police force in question refuses to record a complaint, the Authority will hold informal discussions with the force. If this fails, the Authority has no power to take any further action.

Powers of investigation

The Authority has the power to approve or veto the investigating officer appointed by the police service and to impose reasonable requirements affecting the conduct of the investigation and the use of resources to carry it out.

Criteria for decisions

The standard of proof is the same as in a criminal investigation. All disciplinary charges against a police officer must either be proved *beyond reasonable doubt* or be dismissed.

Confidentiality

As a rule, the Authority does not publish details of individual reports. However, high-profile cases are publicised in press releases - including the name of the police force and, sometimes, the complainant. Cases are sometimes summarised in the *Annual Report.*

Stages in complaint resolution

Preliminary stage

Complainants who contact the Authority before their complaint has been recorded are given advice and guidance, and their complaint is passed through to the force concerned for formal recording (see Exhausting the internal complaints procedure above).

Complaints that are not within the scheme's remit will be referred to a citizens advice bureaux.

Informal resolution

Once a complaint has been recorded and if the complainant would be satisfied with an explanation or an apology, the police force concerned may be able to resolve the complaint informally. The resolution process is carried out by a senior police officer. Complainants who remain dissatisfied can still ask for the complaint to be formally investigated.

Full investigation

If informal resolution is not acceptable to the complainant or the complaint raises serious allegations, it must be fully investigated by a senior police officer from the force concerned. Police forces must notify the most serious complaints to the Authority as soon as they are recorded and the Authority must, by law, supervise all investigations concerning a death or serious injury, and may also choose to investigate other complaints.

Supervised cases

If it is to be a supervised investigation, the Authority appoints one of its own members to take personal responsibility for supervising the case and liaising closely with the investigating police officer. The supervising member reviews the evidence collected during the investigation and can at any time ask for additional enquiries to be carried out. Supervising members can make site visits and meet complainants and community groups.

Statement of satisfaction

After a supervised investigation, the Authority's supervising member issues a statement of satisfaction regarding the criminal and disciplinary aspects of the case. Statements of satisfaction are not always issued, either because the case has been withdrawn or because of non-co-operation by the complainant (in which case the Authority may issue the police force in question with a dispensation from the requirement to investigate).

If there are criminal allegations, the case is referred to the Crown Prosecution Service.

Checking the investigation report

Whether or not it has supervised the case, the Authority examines all reports by an investigating officer, to check that the complaint has been thoroughly investigated and to decide whether any police officers should face disciplinary charges. If there is a formal disciplinary charge, the complainant may be asked to attend the hearing. In rare cases - where a police force disputes the charges and has been directed to hold a disciplinary tribunal - an Authority member will sit on the tribunal. Even if formal disciplinary action is not taken, the officer may still face informal action - such as advice or admonishment.

If no disciplinary action is taken, the complainant will receive a letter from the Authority explaining the outcome of the complaint.

Progress reports

Complainants are informed as each stage of the process is reached.

Types of ruling

Informal resolution

Used for less serious cases, if the complainant agrees (between 30% and 40% of all recorded complaints are dealt with in this way).

Statement of satisfaction

When the Authority has supervised a formal investigation, it issues a statement saying whether or not it is satisfied with the way the investigation was handled and specifying any areas about which it is concerned. (Around 1 in 8 of complaints is supervised.)

Referral for prosecution or disciplinary charges

If it appears that an officer has broken the criminal law, the Authority can refer the case to the Crown Prosecution Service (if the police force concerned has not already done so). If the Crown Prosecution Service decides not to prosecute, the Authority can recommend or direct that the police officer should be charged with a disciplinary offence.

Rights of appeal against a decision

The complainant has no right of appeal within the Authority.

(A member of the police force does have a right of appeal within the disciplinary procedures and cannot be tried on both criminal and disciplinary charges for the same offence.)

Whatever the outcome of a complaint, the complainant keeps the right to bring a civil action against the police.

The Authority is subject to judicial review. There were 5 such reviews in 1995/96 (2 of them referred by the Authority itself); the Authority's decision was upheld in all of them.

Failure to comply with rulings

There have been no failures to comply with Police Complaints Authority recommendations or directions. Directions have statutory force under the Police and Criminal Evidence Act 1984 and therefore are mandatory.

How long does the process take?

Target timescale

120 days for completing an investigation from the date it is referred to the Authority; 28 days for considering completed investigation files.

Actual timescale

58% of Authority-supervised complaints are resolved within 120 days; completed investigation files are considered in an average of 55 days.

Delegation of decision-making

Members of the Authority do not delegate their powers.

Following up complaints

Complaints not within the Authority's remit are not followed up.

Complaining about the scheme itself

Complaints are handled informally by the Authority.

3. The scheme's structure and administration

Origins and membership

A statutory scheme set up under the Police and Criminal Evidence Act 1984. Started operating in May 1985. The Authority oversees and supervises police investigations and reviews police discipline. It is not exactly equivalent to an Ombudsman service, but the Authority's members have some similar functions.

Structure and accountability

The Police Complaints Authority is accountable to parliament through the Home Secretary and is supervised by a Board.

The Authority and its Board

Membership

Chairman, deputy chairman and 11 members. All are lay people and all work full-time for the Authority. Posts are advertised nationally and members appointed by the Home Secretary. Members cannot be serving or ex-members of a police service.

Term of appointment

3 years; eligible for reappointment for a further 3 years.

The Board's role

To oversee policy and day-to-day decision-making. The Board is independent of the Home Office.

The Authority's role

To supervise the investigation of any complaint relating to a death or serious injury; to supervise investigations into non-complaint matters that have been voluntarily referred by police forces because of their potential gravity - for example, shooting incidents, deaths in police custody and cases of serious corruption. (May also call in for supervision any complaint not referred voluntarily); to review the outcome of every investigation, whether supervised or not, and decide whether disciplinary action should be taken against any police officer (if charges have not already been brought); to keep police complaints procedures under review and draw matters of concern to the Home Secretary.

Scheme's terms of reference

These are laid down in the Police and Criminal Evidence Act 1984 and can only be changed by amending legislation.

Monitoring

Standards of service are published in the *Annual Report*. Police forces' responses to Authority recommendations are monitored. Since 1992, the

Authority has conducted annual public attitude surveys: findings are summarised in the *Annual Report*. The Authority is building up a database on the age, ethnic origin and gender of all complainants, together with details of particular factors such as the presence of alcohol and the use of rigid handcuffs, batons or CS spray.

BIOA member?

Yes.

Funding

Funded directly from the Home Office.

Costs

Running cost

£3.8 million in 1995/96 (£3.79 million in 1994/95).

Cost per complaint

Not available.

Staffing

Overall responsibility

The Authority's chairman.

Staff

The Authority's 13 members are directly involved in casework. Staff work in two divisions: One (the deputy chairman, 5 members and 11 case-workers) supervises investigations; the other (the chairman, 6 members and 29 case-workers) deals with disciplinary matters. There are 16 administrative staff.

Forthcoming changes

The Authority has recommended changes to its procedures and powers over the years - to concentrate resources on the most serious complaints - for which it continues to press. The Police and Magistrates Court Act will change the disciplinary procedures.

Improving best practice

Keeps the working of police complaints procedures under review and can make recommendations to the Home Secretary. Issues guidance notes to police forces. Raises general concerns in the media and *Annual Report*. Has contacts with representative organisations.

Facts and figures

Numbers of cases and complaints dealt with by the Authority

Subject of complaint	1994/95	1995/96	% change
Serious non-sexual assault	245	179	-27
Sexual assault	51	46	-10
Other assault	6,318	6,374	1
Oppressive conduct or harassment	1,567	1,437	-8
Unlawful/unnecessary arrest or detention	1,512	1,529	1
Racially discriminatory behaviour	362	397	10
Irregularity in evidence/perjury	758	721	-5
Corrupt practice	127	93	-27
Mishandling of property	604	563	-7
Stop and Search	216	228	6
Searching of premises and seizure of property offence	656	581	-11
Detention, treatment and questioning	1,253	1,280	2
Identification	28	34	21
Tape recording	10	9	-10
Multiple or unspecified code breaches	60	65	8
Failure in duty	1,745	1,772	2
Other procedural irregularity	609	424	-30
Incivility	2,077	2,015	-3
Traffic irregularity	138	122	-12
Other	767	738	-4

Numbers of complaints at each stage of procedure

	1994/95	1995/96	% change
Total complaints and cases dealt with	19,103	18,607	-3
Cases referred to Authority for possible supervision[1]	3,755	2,761	-26
Investigations supervised - involving death or serious injury	574	582	1
Investigations supervised at discretion of Authority - involving actual bodily harm	190	254	34
Investigations supervised at discretion of Authority - involving corruption	22	29	32
Investigations supervised at discretion of Authority - involving a serious arrestable offence	37	58	57
Complaints voluntarily referred and accepted for supervision	48	103	115
Referral for supervision required by Authority	17	6	-65
Dispensation from requirement to investigate granted to police force	7,917	8,873	12

Outcome of cases formally investigated

	1994/95	1995/96	% change
Criminal charges brought by Crown Prosecution Service	34	16	-
Informal disciplinary action	908	827	-
Formal disciplinary charges	288	213	-
No disciplinary action (insufficient or conflicting evidence, officer no longer serving or already subject to criminal charges)	9,907	8,694	-

[1] Note that these are the cases actually accepted for supervision. Except for death or serious injury, where virtually all cases are accepted, considerably more cases are referred than are actually accepted.

Information available about the scheme

Publicising the scheme

A leaflet about the scheme is available in citizens advice bureaux, law centres and police stations.

Terms of reference

Summarised in the *Annual Report*.

Annual Report

> Usually published in July. In addition to the tables above, includes information on historic trends, detailed breakdowns of informal resolutions, caseloads, allegations made where persons were arrested under emergency legislation, and financial accounts.
>
> Also publishes guidance notes for police forces; case summaries; press notices.

Other publications

> Police Complaints Authority, *Police Complaints Authority - The First Ten Years*, HMSO, 1995.

Independent Commission for Police Complaints in Northern Ireland

Chamber of Commerce House, 22 Great Victoria Street, Belfast BT2 7LP
Tel: 01232 244821. Fax: 01232 248563

Chairman: Paul Donnelly
Chief Executive: Brian McClelland

1. Using the scheme: key points

Service-providers covered

Members of the Royal Ulster Constabulary, including reserve members.

The Larne Harbour Police, Ministry of Defence Police, Northern Ireland Airport Constabulary and the Belfast Harbour Police.

Complaints covered

Complaints about the conduct of a police officer below the rank of assistant chief constable, including:

- incivility;

- irregularities in relation to evidence, police procedure or searching premises;

- assault;

- corrupt or discriminatory practice.

Complaints not covered

Ministerial decisions.

Complaints about the general administration, efficiency and procedures of a police force.

Complaints against a police officer above the rank of chief superintendent.

Who can complain?

Private individuals or groups of individuals (not businesses, charities, or other unincorporated bodies).

Friends, relatives, MPs and legal representatives on behalf of an individual.

Friends, relatives and legal representatives on behalf of a dead person.

Cost

Free to complainants.

Geographical limits

The scheme covers police forces in Northern Ireland only.

Complainants do not have to be resident in Northern Ireland.

Time limits

Complaints must reach the scheme within 12 months of the incident that gave rise to the complaint. This time limit can be waived if there is good reason for the delay.

Remedies

Financial compensation

The Commission cannot award financial compensation: for this, the complainant has to bring a civil action for damages in court.

Other

The Commission can recommend informal disciplinary action or disciplinary charges against the officer concerned. A review of police force policy. He can also recommend that an explanation or apology be given.

2. The complaints procedure

Making the complaint

Applicants can complain directly to the Commission, or go to any police station or contact the Police Authority for Northern Ireland. Complaints should be in writing, but an oral complaint is acceptable to start the process. There is no standard complaint form, but there is a guidance leaflet (including a braille version).

Exhausting the internal complaints procedure

The complaint must be recorded by the police force concerned before an investigation can begin, but the complainant does not have to exhaust any internal police complaints procedure before using the scheme.

Powers of investigation

The Commission has the power to approve or veto the investigating officer appointed by the police service and to impose reasonable requirements for the conduct of the investigation and the use of resources employed to carry it out. When reviewing disciplinary matters, the Commission can, if dissatisfied with the investigation, request further information.

Criteria for decisions

The standard of proof is the same as in a criminal investigation. All disciplinary charges against a police officer must either be proved *beyond reasonable doubt* or be dismissed.

Confidentiality

The Commission does not publish details of individual reports.

Noteworthy cases are published in the *Annual Report*, the parties are sometimes identified.

Stages in complaint resolution

Preliminary stage

Whether the complaint is received first by the Commission or by the police, it is referred to the RUC Complaints and Discipline Department - which in turn refers it for informal resolution by a senior police officer, if appropriate.

Complaints that are not within the scheme's remit are automatically forwarded to the chief constable or the police authority, as appropriate.

Informal resolution

A report is submitted to the Commission for review. Complainants who remain dissatisfied can still ask for the complaint to be formally investigated.

Full investigation

A complaint that is not suitable for informal resolution is passed to the Commission, which decides whether or not it will supervise the investigation.

Supervised cases

If it is to be a supervised investigation, the Commission appoints one of its own members to take personal responsibility for the supervision and to liaise closely with the investigating police officer. The supervising member reviews the evidence collected during the investigation and at any time can ask for additional enquiries to be made. Supervising members attend the majority of interviews with complainants and accused officers.

Statement of satisfaction

After a supervised investigation, the Commission's supervising member issues a statement of satisfaction regarding the criminal and disciplinary aspects of the case. Statements of satisfaction are not always issued, either because the case has been withdrawn or because of non-co-operation by the complainant (in which case the Commission may issue the police force in question with a dispensation from the requirement to investigate).

If there are criminal allegations, the case is referred to the Director of Public Prosecutions.

Checking the investigation report

Whether or not the case has been supervised, the case report is referred to the Assistant Chief Constable and then to the Commission for a decision on what disciplinary steps should be taken: no disciplinary action, informal disciplinary action, or a formal disciplinary charge. If the Commission directs (rather than merely recommends) that a disciplinary charge should be brought, two Commission members will sit on the disciplinary tribunal chaired by the chief constable.

Decisions on disciplinary action are communicated to the complainant - by the police if a formal disciplinary charge is brought, and by the Commission in other cases.

Progress reports

Complainants are informed as each stage of the process is reached.

Types of ruling

Informal resolution

Used, with the complainant's consent, in cases where the conduct complained about would not, even if proved, justify a criminal or disciplinary charge. (Used in 37% of all complaints that were fully investigated in 1996.)

Statement of satisfaction

When the Commission has supervised a formal investigation, it issues a statement saying whether it is satisfied with how the investigation was handled (15% of all investigations were supervised in 1996).

Referral for prosecution or disciplinary charges

If it seems that an officer has broken the criminal law, the Commission can refer the case to the Director of Public Prosecutions (DPP) if the police force concerned has not already done so. If the DPP decides not to prosecute, the Commission can recommend or direct (in consultation with the assistant chief constable) that the police officer be charged with a disciplinary offence.

Rights of appeal against a decision

The complainant has no right of appeal within the Commission.

(A member of the police force involved in disciplinary action does have a right of appeal within the disciplinary procedures.)

Whatever the outcome of a complaint, the complainant keeps the right to bring a civil action against the police.

The Commission is subject to judicial review. There have been 4 such reviews in the scheme's lifetime (mostly concerned with the Commission's decision to bring disciplinary charges).

Failure to comply with rulings

There have been no failures to comply with the Commission's directions. Should there be a failure to comply, the Commission would issue a negative Statement of Satisfaction in supervised cases.

How long does the process take?

Not given.

Delegation of decision-making

Members of the Commission do not delegate powers.

Following up complaints

Complaints not within the Commission's remit are not followed up.

Complaining about the scheme itself

Complaints are handled informally by the Commission. Complainants can also write to the Northern Ireland Office.

3. The scheme's structure and administration

Origins and membership

A statutory scheme set up under the Police (Northern Ireland) Order 1987. Started operating on 29 February 1988. The Commission provides an independent element in the handling of complaints against the police in Northern Ireland, by supervising police investigations and reviewing police discipline. It is not exactly equivalent to an Ombudsman service, but the Commission's members have similar functions.

Structure and accountability

The Commission reports to the Secretary of State for Northern Ireland.

The Commission

Membership

A chairman, 2 deputy chairmen and 6 members. Cannot be serving or ex-members of a police service. All work part-time, except for one full-time deputy chairman. Appointed by the Secretary of State.

Term of appointment

3 years, eligible for reappointment.

Role

To supervise the investigation of any complaint alleging that a member of the police service caused a death or serious injury (has the option to supervise formal investigation of any other complaints against the police); to decide whether a police officer who is the subject of a complaint should be charged with an offence against police discipline, if such a charge has not already been brought; to oversee the procedure for dealing with less serious complaints by way of an informal resolution; to keep under review the working of police complaints procedures and review them once every 3 years. Can draw matters of concern to the attention of the Secretary of State. Appoints the scheme's chief executive. Meets monthly.

Scheme's terms of reference

These are laid down in the Police (Northern Ireland) Order 1987 and can only be changed by amending legislation.

Monitoring

Standards of service are published in the *Annual Report*. Conducts routine monitoring of complainants' satisfaction and periodic surveys of complainants which are summarised in the *Annual Report*.

BIOA member?

Yes.

Funding

Funded directly from the Northern Ireland Office.

Costs

Running costs

£780,000 in 1995/96 (£781,000 in 1994/95).

Cost per complaint

Not given.

Staffing

Overall responsibility

The chief executive.

Staff

The 9 Commission members are directly involved in casework. There are 9 caseworkers (some legally qualified), divided into a discipline section and a supervision section, and 5 administrative staff.

Forthcoming changes

The Commission's two triennial reviews resulted in a number of recommendations some of which have not, as yet, been accepted by the Secretary of State. The Commission continues to press for their implementation. A fundamental review of the scheme was carried out in 1995/96 by Dr Maurice Hayes. He reported in January 1997 recommending that there should be a Police Ombudsman responsible to Parliament with a duty to investigate complaints and to report his/her findings.

Improving best practice

The Commission keeps the working of police complaints procedures under review and makes a report to the Secretary of State every 3 years.

Facts and figures

Numbers of allegations received (including telephone complaints)[1]

Subject of complaint	1995	1996
Assault	1,113	820
Corrupt practice	12	3
Discriminatory behaviour	6	1
Incivility	418	307
Irregularity in relation to evidence	25	9
Irregularity in police procedure	229	168
Irregularity in search of premises	44	32
Mishandling of property	31	17
Neglect of duty	127	104
Oppressive conduct/harassment	196	148
Traffic offence	11	10
Unlawful arrest/detention	104	91
Miscellaneous crime	55	41
Miscellaneous other/discipline	14	18

[1] Note that a single complaint can contain several allegations.

Number of complaints at each stage of procedure

	1995	1996
New complaints received	2,328	2,540
Informal resolutions	566	648
Cases referred for possible supervision	2,330	2,544
Investigations supervised (involving death or serious injury)	84	140
Investigations supervised at discretion of Commission	281	250
Cases withdrawn during investigation	50	71
Dispensation from requirement to investigate granted to police force	46	61
Statement issued	214	259

Outcome of cases formally investigated

Informal disciplinary action initiated by Commission	50	33
Informal disciplinary action initiated by RUC	94	120
Formal disciplinary charges initiated by Commission (guilty finding)	1	--
Formal disciplinary charges initiated by Commission (not guilty/dismissed)	13	7
Formal disciplinary charges initiated by RUC (guilty finding)	4	14
Formal disciplinary charges initiated by RUC (not guilty/dismissed)	4	18
No disciplinary action	1,206	911

Information available about the scheme

Publicising the scheme

A leaflet about the scheme (including a braille version) is available in citizens advice bureaux, public libraries, law centres, social security offices and police stations. A video is also available.

The Commission's chairman takes part in press and media interviews. The scheme also takes part in police training, and during recent years has visited district councils and schools.

Terms of reference

Summarised in the *Annual Report* and leaflet.

Annual Report

Usually published in April. As well as the tables above, it includes information on historic trends, detailed breakdowns of informal resolutions, caseloads, allegations made where persons were arrested under emergency legislation, and financial accounts.

Other publications

Community Opinion Survey 1996 (unpublished). The findings are summarised in the 1996 *Annual Report.*

Police

Adjudicator for Inland Revenue, Customs and Excise and Contributions Agency

Haymarket House, 28 Haymarket, London SW1Y 4SP
Tel: 0171 930 2292. Fax: 0171 930 2298

Adjudicator: Elizabeth Filkin

1. Using the scheme: key points

Service-providers covered

Inland Revenue (including the Valuation Office Agency), Customs and Excise, and the Contributions Agency.

Complaints covered

Complaints about the way a department has handled someone's affairs - for instance, mistakes, delays, behaviour of staff/departmental procedures or the use of discretion in making an individual decision.

Complaints not covered

Ministerial decisions.

Appeals against:

- property valuations by the Valuation Office Agency;

- tax assessments and other matters that can be handled by the General or Special Commissioners of the Inland Revenue;

- matters that can be handled by VAT and customs duties tribunals.

Disputes on matters of law relating to the complainant's national insurance liability (on which there is a right of appeal to the Secretary of State for Social Security).

Complaints already investigated by the Parliamentary Ombudsman.

Cases on which a court has already ruled or which are already subject to court proceedings.

The scheme does not deal with matters relating to a criminal prosecution brought by the department concerned until the completion of all court proceedings.

Who can complain?

Private individuals, partnerships, charities, unincorporated bodies, companies and businesses.

An agent, such as an accountant or solicitor, on someone else's behalf, with that person's permission.

An agent, such as an accountant or solicitor, on behalf of a dead person.

Cost

Free to complainants.

Geographical limits

United Kingdom except for the Contributions Agency, which does not cover Northern Ireland at present, but soon will.

Time limits

Complaints must usually reach the Adjudicator not more than 6 months after a senior staff member in the department concerned has replied to the complaint.

The problem must have arisen after:

- April 1993 for the Inland Revenue and Valuation Office Agency;

- April 1995 for Customs and Excise and the Contributions Agency.

The Adjudicator can decide to deal with complaints outside these time limits.

Remedies

Financial compensation

Can include payment for financial loss, and worry and distress. No formal maximum: the Adjudicator can recommend any amount in line with whatever the departments' own codes of practice require them to consider. (Average compensation in 1995/96, £800 for Inland Revenue and Customs and Excise cases, and around £60 for Contributions Agency cases. The highest award was £28,490, in an Inland Revenue case.)

Can, a nd often does, recommend the reimbursement of costs (including professional fees), incurred by the complainant because of serious error by a department.

Can recommend that interest is paid as part of the award.

Other

Can recommend corrective action. Examples include correcting or waiving the complainant's liability, and/or recommending that a department reviews practice, changes a procedure, or issues an apology.

2. The complaints procedure

Making the complaint

Complainants can approach the scheme direct or be referred by the department concerned, an accountant, a lawyer, an MP, the press, friends or relatives. A complaint can be made in any form. It does not have to be in writing and there is no standard complaints form. Guidance leaflets - one each for the Inland Revenue, Customs and Excise and the Contributions Agency - are available (in many different language versions) and the scheme will provide translation and interpreters. There are braille and audio-tape versions of the leaflet for complaints about Customs and Excise.

Exhausting the internal complaints procedure

Complainants do not need to have exhausted a department's internal complaints procedure before approaching the scheme. However, the

Adjudicator sees the scheme's first task as helping people to try to resolve their complaints through internal complaints systems. Where appropriate, before she starts a full investigation, she will help complainants contact the department concerned to give it a chance to resolve the matter.

The Adjudicator will intervene earlier if there is good reason.

Powers of investigation

The Adjudicator has complete access to the departments' papers and staff. Staff can be asked to attend hearings and the Adjudicator expects the departments to ensure their attendance.

Criteria for decisions

The evidence in the particular case, taking into account codes of practice, internal instructions, behaviour, courtesy and whether the department concerned acted fairly and consistently.

The Adjudicator is not bound by the scheme's previous decisions or by legal precedent.

Confidentiality

During an investigation, no correspondence is routinely copied to the other party except, usually, the draft summary of factual events.

Noteworthy cases are summarised in an anonymised form in quarterly reports to the departments and in the *Annual Report*. Nothing is disclosed that could identify the complainant or another member of the public. The departments concerned are named.

Stages in complaint resolution

Assistance

Complaints come into the scheme's assistance unit first. If the complainant has not already used the internal complaints system of the department concerned, the complaint is called an assistance case: the Adjudicator's office helps the complainant to clarify the complaint and asks the department to review it at senior level. If a case is not within the scheme's remit, the complainant is referred back to the department and, if appropriate, told of the tribunal or appeal body that can deal with the complaint.

Investigation and hearings

When a case is taken up for investigation, the scheme obtains details of the complaint from the complainant, and asks for a report and all papers from the appropriate office of the department in question. The papers are reviewed and, usually, a summary of events is prepared. The summary of events is often sent in draft to both parties to be checked for factual accuracy. Some cases can be decided on the written evidence. Sometimes staff also interview one or both sides, or third parties, and the Adjudicator may hold hearings (at an appropriate location). Further information is gathered where necessary, and mediation is considered.

Recommendation

If mediation is not suitable or successful, a formal letter of recommendation goes to the complainant, copied to the department.

Progress reports

There is no fixed procedure, but the scheme makes sure it keeps in contact with the complainant.

Types of ruling

Mediation

About 40% of investigated cases reach an agreed settlement as a result of mediation.

Formal recommendation

Just over half of investigated cases have been completed with a formal recommendation.

The remaining cases have either been withdrawn by complainants during the investigation (6% overall) or reconsidered by the departments concerned (3% overall).

Rights of appeal against a decision

The scheme has its own complaints procedure, allowing complainants to tell the Adjudicator if they are not satisfied with her recommendation.

There is no external appeal procedure but after a complaint has been dealt with by the Adjudicator, it can still be referred to the Parliamentary Ombudsman (see separate entry on page 69).

The scheme is subject to judicial review. (One application for review has been made so far: it was refused.)

Failure to comply with rulings

The three departments have agreed to accept the Adjudicator's recommendations in all but exceptional circumstances (and have so far accepted all recommendations). If a department did refuse to accept a recommendation, the Adjudicator could use a press announcement to publicise its refusal.

How long does the process take?

Target timescale

4 and a half months for investigation cases.

Actual timescale

4 and a half months for investigation cases.

Complaints may be given priority if there is an urgent issue, such as an imminent bankruptcy action or repossession.

Delegation of decision-making

There is no deputy Adjudicator. The Adjudicator personally signs every letter of recommendation. The Adjudicator's powers to seek a mediated settlement (where appropriate) are delegated to the scheme's Adjudication Officers.

Following up complaints

Cases not within the scheme's remit are not followed up. When a complaint is referred back to the department in question, the department usually provides the Adjudicator with a copy of its response to the complainant. When the Adjudicator has made a recommendation, the department provides a copy of its response to the complainant. The Adjudicator asks for information on action following every complaint where she finds something wrong, and comments on the quality of the action.

Complaining about the scheme itself

There is a procedure for dealing with complaints about the scheme. Complaints are handled by the Adjudicator. (One complaint has been upheld.)

3. The scheme's structure and administration

Origins and membership

Set up by the Inland Revenue in 1993 as part of its efforts to improve customer service. Customs and Excise and the Contributions Agency joined in 1995.

Structure and accountability

The Adjudicator has a personal contract with each of the 3 government departments/agencies covered by the scheme.

The departments

Role

The boards of the Inland Revenue, Customs and Excise and the Contributions Agency have each undertaken to provide the Adjudicator with support to help her with her duties, and to consult her about the management, staffing and administration of the Adjudicator's office. Her contract gives her sole discretion, free of any directive by the departments. They play no role in the resolution of complaints.

The Adjudicator

Appointment

By the board of Inland Revenue, the board of Customs and Excise and the board of the Contributions Agency. Can be terminated only on grounds of gross misconduct.

Term of appointment

Initially 3 years, no restrictions on reappointment.

Role

Responsible for running the office and complaints-handling.

Scheme's terms of reference

Set out in the Adjudicator's contracts with the departments. Can be changed by mutual agreement.

Monitoring

Standards of service are published in the *Annual Report*. A range of customer surveys is conducted annually and findings summarised in the *Annual Report*.

BIOA member?

Associate member.

Funding

The three departments meet the costs of the Adjudicator's office, in proportion to the estimated number of likely complaints.

Costs

Running cost

Forecast for 1996/97 - £1,761,000.

Actual cost

In 1995/96 - £1,422,718.

Staffing

Day-to-day management

The responsibility of the Head of Office and 6 managers.

Staff

45 staff in all, divided into 5 adjudication teams and an assistance team, each under a manager. (Some staff are legally qualified, others have a background as accountants, advice workers, civil servants or local government officers.)

Forthcoming changes

No major changes expected.

Improving best practice

The Adjudicator and her staff encourage good practice by circulating newsletters, attending conferences held by the departments and visiting their local and regional offices.

Quarterly information is provided to the departments and the Adjudicator meets their senior managements regularly. Service initiatives introduced by the departments in response to the Adjudicator's criticisms are listed in the *Annual Report*.

Facts and figures

New complaints received in 1995/96 (% change over 1994/95 in brackets)[1]

	Inland Revenue	
Cause of complaint	**Investigations**	**Assistance**
Mistakes	145	(-20%) 386
Delay	71	(0%) 452
Superficial work	11	(-17%) 24
Attitude of staff	36	(-22%) 84
Departmental procedures	36	(9%) 364
Organisational failures	2	2
Failure to keep taxpayer informed	11	(-6%) 43
No liaison within Department	3	(-3%) 30
Use of discretion	107	(-26%) 206
Abuse of powers	2	2
Wrong advice	26	(-17%) 29
Open government	2	2
Other	33	(44%) 410

	Customs and Excise	
Cause of complaint	**Investigations**	**Assistance**
Mistakes	13	65
Delay	6	89
Superficial work	2	2
Attitude of staff	15	34
Departmental procedures	2	2
Organisational failures	5	79
Failure to keep taxpayer informed	2	2
No liaison within Department	2	2
Use of discretion	19	145
Abuse of powers	1	1
Wrong advice	2	2
Open government	6	47
Other	13	115

Contributions Agency

Cause of complaint	Investigations	Assistance
Mistakes	5	13
Delay	5	23
Superficial work	2	2
Attitude of staff	2	3
Departmental procedures	5	11
Organisational failures	2	2
Failure to keep taxpayer informed	1	8
No liaison within Department	0	1
Use of discretion	2	2
Abuse of powers	2	2
Wrong advice	1	6
Open government	2	2
Other	1	22

[1] The Scheme was only extended to Customs and Excise in April 1995, and the Contributions Agency in June 1995. Percentage changes are not given for Inland Revenue investigation cases because the numbers are small and show very little change. Note that figures include telephone complaints.
[2] Subject category not applicable.

Numbers of complaints at each stage of procedure in year to 31/3/96 (% change over 1994-95 in brackets)[1]

	Inland Revenue	Customs and Excise	Contributions Agency
Total complaints received	2,507 (-3%)	653	107
Assistance cases received	2,028 (-2%)	575	87
Investigation cases received	479 (-5%)	78	20

Outcome of investigation cases completed

Complaint not upheld	228[2]	15	2
Complaint upheld wholly or substantially	145[2]	8	8
Complaint upheld in part	94[2]	17	2
Complaint withdrawn	28[2]	6	1

[1] The Scheme was only extended to Customs and Excise in April 1995, and to the Contributions Agency in June 1995.
[2] Percentage changes are not given because in previous years no distinction was made between cases upheld in part and cases upheld wholly or substantially.

Information available about the scheme

Publicising the scheme

The scheme is publicised through the departments' own complaints leaflets and their codes of practice. It is also mentioned on tax and VAT return forms. Leaflets are available from the Adjudicator's office, local offices of departments covered by the scheme, citizens advice bureaux, law centres, embassies, etc.

The scheme maintains contacts with the media and a wide range of organisations and individuals.

Terms of reference

Published in the press release on the appointment of the Adjudicator, and summarised in the scheme leaflets.

Annual Report

Usually published in September/October. In addition to the tables above, includes detailed breakdowns by subject of complaint, departmental offices/units involved in complaints, the outcome of investigation cases completed and a financial overview.

Other publications

Public Service Committee, Third Report, *The Citizen's Charter*, HMSO, March 1997.

Philip Morris, 'The Revenue Adjudicator - The First Two Years', *Public Law*, Sweet & Maxwell, 1996.

Also publishes quarterly reports to the departments. They comprise guidance notes for the departments, free-standing case summaries and statistics.